HOW TO BUILD

COLLECTIBLE BIRDHOUSES

Radnor-Hill Publishing, Inc.
Philadelphia

HOW TO BUILD

COLLECTIBLE

BIRDHOUSES

HEIRLOOMS FOR YOUR GREAT GRANDCHILDREN AND OTHER LOVED ONES

HOW TO TURN ANY STRUCTURE, REAL OR IMAGINED, INTO A BIRDHOUSE

DAVID KEPHART

TABLE OF CONTENTS

HOW TO TURN ANY STRUCTURE INTO A BIRDHOUSE

READY TO USE PLANS

ARCHITECTURAL REPLICA PLANS

PLANS BY MALCOLM WELLS

PLANS BY GLADSTONE CALIFF

NOW THAT YOU HAVE BUILT A BIRDHOUSE

INTRODUCTION

There are a lot of books out there that tell you how to build average birdhouses. But you're probably not average. You want a little more from life and you're willing to put a little more into your birdhouse project. That's what this book is about — making your birdhouse a creation of your heart as well as a shelter for your feathery friends.

You need only the most basic woodworking skills (or be willing to learn them) to design and build a birdhouse using the methods in this book.

Throughout the book, I refer to hand tools.

If you prefer power tools, you'll get straighter cuts and such. But you may miss a few whispers of inspiration which are drowned out by the whirring of electric motors and spinning blades.

Although I have included some fun plans in the book, I urge you to try my methods for making your own plans from your own house or any structure that has meaning for you. You can even work from old snapshots of Grandma's farm. If you feel it in your heart, you'll do a fine job. The birds don't care if you're a little off here and there. Grandma wouldn't either.

WHY BUILD A BIRDHOUSE?

Birdhouses are becoming more popular than ever before. It's no surprise. Birds have always brought us joy with their songs, their colorful feathers, their playful ways and the work they do around our yards and gardens. Building a birdhouse is one way to keep the birds around us, and to say thanks for all the happiness they bring us.

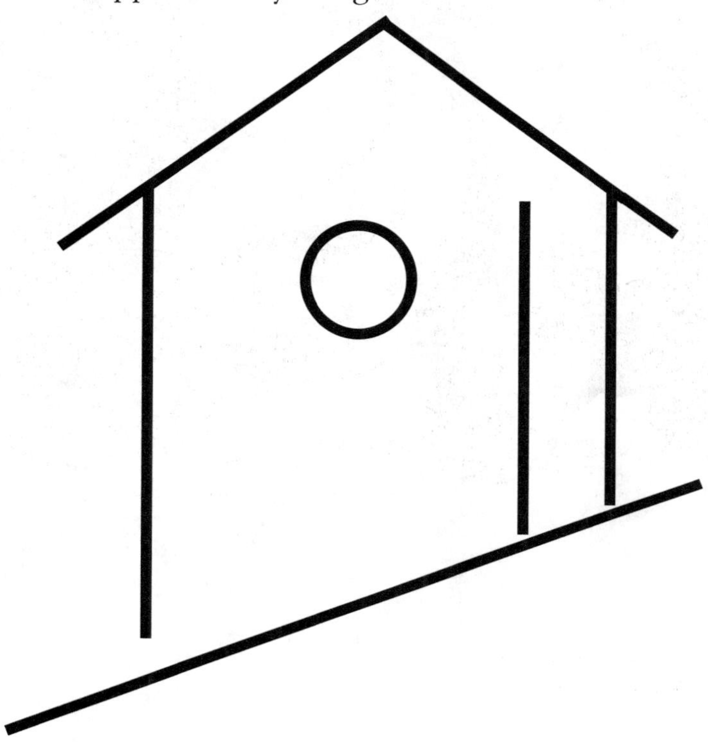

Building a birdhouse is also an excellent way to drain away the stress that builds up during the day in your job or at school. There are few creative activities more immediately rewarding than working nature's materials with your hands.

When you build a birdhouse you are both builder and artist. The builder is rational and ordered, keeping track of dimensions, specifications and procedures. The artist is a dreamer who captures a fleeting imagination and channels it through the hands to make a permanent record in the solid world of matter. Your birdhouse project will let you please both sides of your brain in whatever measure seems right to you.

When you are finished with your birdhouse, you will have created an object that is simple and tangible, yet adds value to any home.

More than this, to the extent that you have put your heart into your birdhouse, you will have created an object of immeasurable value to your offspring, who will treasure your creation as an heirloom.

WHAT IS A COLLECTIBLE BIRDHOUSE?

As prices for birdhouses continue to rise, this question pops up constantly at craft shows, flea markets, antique shops, yard sales and gift shops.

What is a collectible birdhouse? The answer depends on the collector.

This birdhouse has spent a lot of time outside, as you can tell from the distressed paint and wood. The worn entrance holes indicate use by birds over the years.

ANTIQUES AND JUST PLAIN OLD

Many collectors are interested in buying old birdhouses which will presumably increase in value over the years. These people want birdhouses which are not only old, but exhibit skilled craftwork, individuality, folk art value, and signs of usage by birds.

Really old working birdhouses are somewhat hard to come by. Birdhouses which are exposed to the elements year after year deteriorate quickly unless they were used in a dry climate or were meticulously maintained.

Obviously you can't build an old birdhouse, even if you use old materials and hardware. But you can pack a lot of craftwork and individuality into your new birdhouse. (Folk art just sort of happens.) Given enough time, your birdhouse will get old on its own.

FOLK ART

Other collectors are looking for birdhouses of any age which are examples of real folk art.

Folk art can be defined as decorative stuff produced by folks (just plain folks, primarily) who have little or no formal training in art.

When you see real folk art, you know it. It communicates a lot of feeling and effort on the artist's part without getting bogged down in trying to be Art (with a capital A).

Folk art often tells a story about the artist's life experience. The story can be as complex as an epic which unfolds as your eyes move across the art. It can also be as simple as the artist saying "this is something like what I see in my mind's eye when I think about that thing."

Being regular folks with regular jobs and all, real folk artists don't study the Masters, speak in hushed tones about Significance, or consciously try to shock you with the New. Ironically, some professional artists who do all of the above on a regular basis try to make their work look like the work of folk artists.

When you build your birdhouse, you'll make folk art if your heart has something to say and your brain doesn't get carried away thinking about what folk art should look like to a "serious" collector. All homemade, hand crafted birdhouses are folk art to some extent.

Birdhouses which are churned out by folk art "factories" are not folk art. They're products made to look like folk art. Copy what you see in your mind's eye, not what you see in a catalog or gift shop.

This folk art mural was painted by a sailor aboard a navy ship. It commemorates a real event and real people.

This birdhouse commemorates an event from my past. It's a mind's-eye approximation of a place that really exists.

These birdhouses are prime examples of folk art. That they have survived to old age is a testament to how well they were loved by their owners.

HIGH DESIGN

A growing number of collectors are looking for birdhouses produced by noted architects, designers and craftspeople.

As birdhouses gain in popularity, many people with talent for designing and building are finding their way toward the birdhouse as a medium for expression.

These people generally have formal training in what constitutes pleasing and functional design, and you can see it in their birdhouses.

This birdhouse was designed by architect Malcolm Wells. His designs are radically different yet functional. They are also visually pleasing and blend well with their environments.

Some of the most collectible of these birdhouses are those designed by architects who apply their knowledge of how housing can be made to blend well in a given environment.

Many of these new architectural designs are radical departures from tradition, yet offer birds solidly functional homes.

If you are inclined to follow this path to your birdhouse project, you will need knowledge of what constitutes good design. This knowledge can be intuitive, meaning you just seem to know what will work, and most of the time it does. Or it can be acquired by studying pictures in books and living examples of good design. The great builders of high design birdhouses usually combine both intuitive and acquired design knowledge.

This birdhouse is a copy of a real house. Unlike the real house, this house can be moved when the family moves — across town or, in 100 years or so, to a colony on Mars.

ARCHITECTURAL REPLICAS

Some collectors have a taste for correctly proportioned copies of existing structures and types of structures.

A spooky Victorian birdhouse may remind one of the type of dwelling he or she would choose if desire outweighed practicality. A birdhouse copy of a humble farm house may spark pleasant memories of a carefree, innocent childhood. For these and many more reasons, architecturally accurate replicas of real structures stir feelings in most people.

If you are interested in building this type of birdhouse, you will find comprehensive help in the section of this book called *How To Turn Any Structure Into A Birdhouse*.

And then there are collectors who are look-ing for birdhouses that just make them (and maybe the birds in their yards) feel good for at least a few minutes every day.

Their tastes are unique. They answer only one qualifying question: "Do I like it?"

Fortunately, for most of us birdhouse builders, the majority of birdhouse collectors (maybe buyers is a better term) make their purchases based on personal taste.

To this great group of collectors, birdhouse value is not established through speculation of financial gain. Instead of money, value is measured in emotion.

They don't get much simpler than this. But even the simplest design can be charming.

What is a collectible birdhouse?

In its most basic form, a collectible birdhouse makes you feel something in your heart when you look at it. And if the builder has put imagination, effort and love into it, the beholder will certainly feel something.

GETTING STARTED

Before you start cutting lumber, you need to ask yourself a few questions. The questions are easy.

All you really need to know is why you're building a birdhouse and what, roughly, you want the finished product to look like.

WHY BUILD A BIRDHOUSE?

Most people say: "to attract birds to my yard and give them a place to nest." This is a great reason! Birds are fun to watch and listen to, and they work like nature's perfect "insecticide" — perfect because they work only on bugs and leave the rest of the environment just as it should be. More birds in your yard and garden means more fun and fewer insects. If this appeals to you, the steward of the earth that lives in you is trying to tell you something.

Then there are people who want to make a three-dimensional record of a special place: a childhood house, a workplace, the family farm as it looked years before the real estate developer plowed it under. If this appeals to you, the artist that lives in you is trying to tell you something.

Some people want to combine both stewardship of the earth and artistic urges. This combination is the seed of effort that makes birdhouses which are fun to look at and useful to the birds.

> *If you've read this far, you probably already have a good idea of what you want to do with your birdhouse project.*

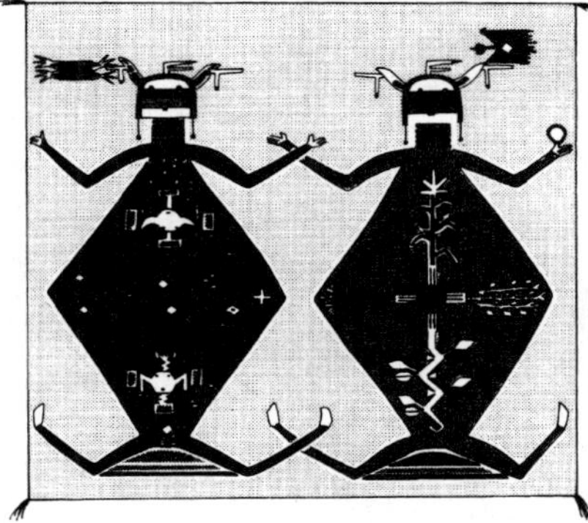

Mother Earth and Father Sky from a Navajo design.

The spark of artistic inspiration.

One more thing. Before you start cutting lumber, you should get familiar with the materials, tools and techniques you'll be using. If you're already an accomplished woodworker, you may still want to look at the *Materials* section

A HOUSE FOR BIRDS, PEOPLE OR BOTH?

Who are you building this house for? This is important. Your answer to this question will help you select the best materials, tools and construction techniques. There are three basic types of birdhouses.

1. Purely functional. If you are building a birdhouse only as a place for birds to use as a nesting shelter, you have the most straightforward job. Looks are not an issue. Just usefulness. But you should pay particular attention to things like dimensions, drainage, ventilation, exterior color and types of building materials. Birds are very sensitive to all of these things.

American Primitive Gallery

2. Purely decorative. If you are building a birdhouse that will spend its days brightening up the inside of a people-house, you can take some liberties with the functional stuff, and use your energy to make it an *objet d'art*, as they say in France.

3. Decorative and functional. If you want a birdhouse that looks like a peoplehouse but has all the functional qualities a real birdhouse needs, you have the most challenging job. You will have to make sure your birdhouse meets all of the functional needs outlined in item 1 above. You can cut some corners on the artistic details, though. When your birdhouse is installed in the yard or garden, its distance from onlookers will hide a multitude of artistic shortcuts.

Most birds are somewhat finicky when they are home shopping. They know their dream house when they see it, and they usually won't settle for less. Still, birds have fairly simple housing needs. As long as the entrance hole and the nesting area are the right size, and the location is good, you'll probably attract the bird family you want.

The *Birdhouse Sizing Guide* in this book gives some guidelines to the dimensions birds are looking for in a house.

Keep in mind that birds are very particular about their habitat as well as their houses. In general, you should have no problem if you are building for birds you have seen around your neighborhood.

If you are trying to attract a species you have not seen around the neighborhood, look at the section called *Location*.

BIRDHOUSE SIZING GUIDE

	NESTING AREA WIDTH, DEPTH, HEIGHT; IN INCHES	ENTRANCE SIZE, HEIGHT ABOVE FLOOR TO CENTER OF HOLE; IN INCHES	MOUNTING HEIGHT; IN INCHES
Bluebird	5 x 5 x 8-12	1-1/2, 6-10	4-6 ft
Chickadee	4 x 4 x 8-10	1-1/8, 6-8	4-15 ft
Flicker	7 x 7 x 16-18	2-1/2, 14-16	6-20 ft
Flycatcher, Ash throated	6 x 6 x 8-12	1-1/2, 6-10	5-15 ft
Flycatcher, Great crested	6 x 6 x 8-12	1-3/4, 6-10	5-15 ft
Nuthatch, Brown headed, Pygmy, and Red breasted	4 x 4 x 8-10	1-1/4, 6-8	5-15 ft
Nuthatch, White breasted	4 x 4 x 8-10	1-3/8, 6-8	5-15 ft
Owl, Barn	10 x 18 x 15-18	6, 4	12-18 ft
Owl, Screech	8 x 8 x 12-15	3, 9-12	10-30 ft
Purple Martin	6 x 6 x 6	2-1/4, 2	6-20 ft
Swallow, Tree and Violet-Green	5 x 5 x 6-8	1-1/2, 4-6	5-15 ft
Titmouse	4 x 4 x 10-12	1-1/4, 6-10	5-15 ft
Warbler, Prothonotary	5 x 5 x 6	1-1/8, 4-5	4-8 ft
Wood Duck	10 x 18 x 10-24	4, 12-16	10-20 ft
Woodpecker, Downy	4 x 4 x 8-10	1-1/4, 6-8	5-15 ft
Woodpecker, Hairy	6 x 6 x 12-15	1-1/2, 9-12	8-20 ft
Woodpecker, Lewis'	7 x 7 x 16-18	2-1/2, 14-16	12-20 ft
Woodpecker, Pileated	8 x 8 x 16-24	3 x 4, 12-20	15-25 ft
Woodpecker, Red headed	6 x 6 x 12-15	2, 9-12	10-20 ft
Yellow Bellied Sapsucker	5 x 5 x 12-15	1-1/2, 9-12	10-20 ft
Wren, Carolina	4 x 4 x 6-8	1-1/2, 4-6	5-10 ft
Wren, House and Berwick's	4 x 4 x 6-8	1-1/4, 4-6	5-10 ft

MATERIALS, TOOLS AND TECHNIQUES

A lot of the character your birdhouse ends up with depends on the materials you choose as well as the design.

This section gives you some guidelines on which materials have been proven in use during the history of birdhouses.

You can substitute materials not listed here. Use common sense. Always keep safety in mind — for you and other people, and for the birds. Also make sure the materials you choose will provide comfort for your bird guests.

BASIC MATERIALS

Wood. It's the best stuff on earth to use in great birdhouses. Wood comes in two basic varieties: solid lumber and plywood.

Solid lumber and plywood are both useful in most birdhouse projects. I recommend using solid 1 X 8 or 1 X 10 for the main structural parts of each birdhouse, and 1/4" plywood for the roof and other non-structural parts.

You'll see in the *Architectural Replica Plans* I've included in this book how I mix solid wood and plywood for best results.

When it comes to mixing types of wood, there is only one rule: if you live in a damp or rainy climate and the birdhouse will be outside, try to use wood that is resistant to moisture. There's more about this in the section called *Wood Types*.

If your birdhouse is for decorative purposes only, you're free to build with anything that works for you. Papier-mache, tongue depressors, cardboard, squashed aluminum cans, concrete... you name it.

When you buy plywood for a birdhouse, look for the label. This one tells you that it's exterior grade, "A" on one side, "C" on the other. This is perfectly adequate for birdhouses.

Other materials you might want to have around when you start your project include:

Nails in the following sizes:

- 4d galvanized finish
- 4d galvanized common
- 3/4" 16 and 18 gauge galvanized brads

Wood screws, brass or stainless, in the following sizes:

- # 8 x 1-1/2"
- # 6 x 1-1/4"
- # 6 x 3/4" (good if you're working with 1/2" wood)

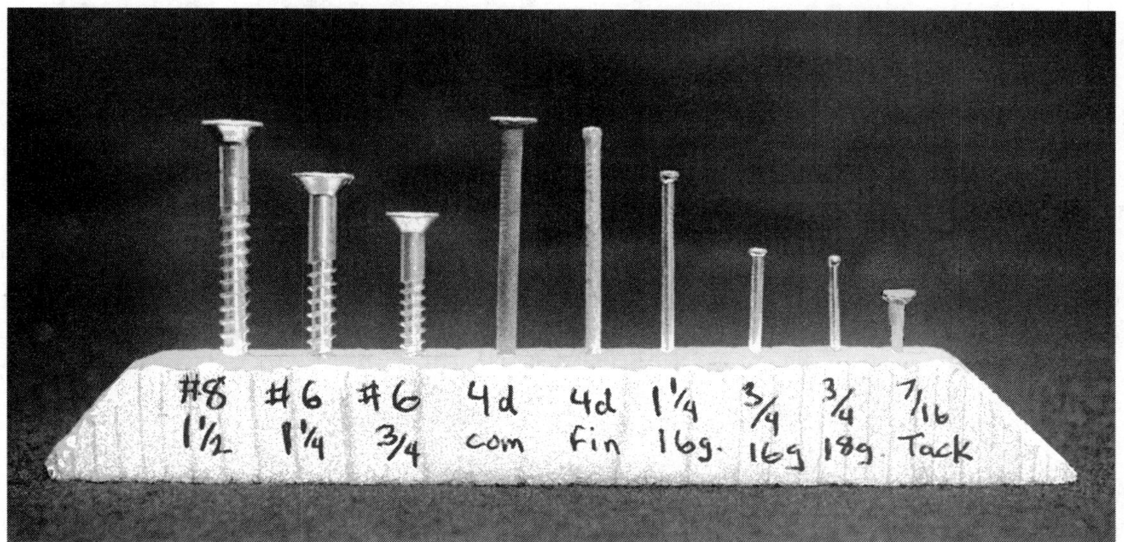

These are the fasteners I use in making birdhouses. Everything is brass, aluminum, copper or galvanized steel.

A good waterproof wood glue. The regular white and yellow wood glue is not going to resist water. There are a number of glues you might consider using:

- Type II weatherproof wood glue is good for attaching large areas where structural strength is required. This is a relatively new product — one part, non toxic and easy to use. Parts joined with this type of glue need to be clamped.

- Hot melt is good for quick, clampless set up where structural strength is not required.

- Epoxy can be used to attach small areas and trim.

Sandpaper, an assortment including 100 and 150 for wood, and 220 and 400 for sanding between coats of paint.

Roofing material. Shingles or roll roofing is good. Ask at your local lumber yard or home center. Or you can just coat a wooden roof with good exterior paint or finish. You can also use sheet metal — galvanized steel, copper or aluminum flashing. Whatever type of metal roofing you use, make sure you use fasteners — screws or nails — made of the same metal. Otherwise corrosion will occur where two different metals touch.

> **CAUTION:** SHEET METAL, SHINGLES AND ROLL ROOFING SHOULD ALWAYS BE APPLIED OVER A WOOD UNDERLAYMENT IN BIRDHOUSES WHICH WILL BE USED AS A SHELTER FOR BIRDS. RADIANT HEAT FROM METAL OR ROOFING MATERIAL CAN BE HARMFUL TO BIRDS.

Trim. There are no rules when it comes to trim. Your best bet is to go to a well-stocked lumber yard or home center and see if anything looks like it belongs on your birdhouse. If you need something extra delicate or fancy, check out a dollhouse supply store. In fact, check out the dollhouse supply store even if you don't need anything in particular. You'll come away with a lot of new ideas. You'll probably also come away with a small paper bag full of things you didn't know existed.

This is some of the dollhouse trim I keep around my shop for emergencies.

WOOD TYPES

You can make a good birdhouse out of just about any untreated, unfinished wood you find or buy.

It's always a good idea to recycle "found" wood. So if you have some or know where to get some, saw it up and make a birdhouse out of it, and don't worry about meeting some exact specification. Just make sure it's not chemically treated or otherwise contaminated.

These are grape crates. There's enough wood in two of these to make a decent birdhouse.

"FOUND" WOOD

I refer to "found" wood throughout this section. What is it? It's any wood that sits around in the basement, garage, or worse, in the trash heap waiting to go to the landfill or incinerator.

We waste tremendous amounts of wood in our society. Once you get tuned in to waste wood, you'll see it everywhere.

Great sources of found wood are houses and barns which are being torn down. Good found wood can also be found (!) in fruit crates, furniture crates, or other packaging.

The guy I buy fruit from is happy to give me his used grape crates so he doesn't have to throw them away. Out of one grape crate, I get two pine boards, each 5/8" thick, 5-1/2 by 13-1/2" long.

The grape crates I use also contain a generous amount of 1/8" plywood sandwiched between paper. The paper comes off pretty easily and these pieces make good roof underlayments if you have regular roofing material to cover them with. The Green Mountain Ranch in the *Architectural Replica Plans* section of this book is made entirely of recycled grape crates.

If you get fruit crates (or any crates) with labels glued to the ends, soak a towel in hot water and lay it over the label. In about 20 minutes you should be able to remove the label with a 1" putty knife. When the label is gone, wash the remaining glue from the board and let it dry thoroughly before you use it.

One more note about grape crates. Some of the wood tends to be cupped, like the bottom of a boat. If the cupping is not too bad, I use the boards for main structural parts, always keeping the "belly" of the cup to the outside of the structure. If the cupping is real bad, I use the boards for partitions inside the birdhouse.

SOLID WOOD

Solid lumber is satisfying to work with and it is pleasing to the eye and the touch. You have a number of choices when it comes to solid lumber.

If you are building a birdhouse on the cheap, any solid 1" thick (it's actually 3/4" thick) wood will do as long as it's

- dry (not sappy or smelly)

- not coated with paint, varnish or any other finish

- not pressure treated to resist decay

If you want to spend a little more money, you can get some nice "1-by" boards at your local lumber yard or home center. White pine, cypress, redwood, red cedar and yellow poplar all make good birdhouses. Redwood stands up to moisture very well. Although many tropical woods stand up to water best of all, using them puts dents in both the rain forest and your wallet.

When it comes to size, ideally you want your board to be wide enough to get your largest piece from it without the need to join boards.

Keep in mind that actual board sizes are smaller than the "1-by" designation. A typical 1" x 8" board will be about 3/4" x 7-1/4". If you are buying lumber, make sure you know the dimensions of your birdhouse before you go to the lumberyard.

If your found boards are narrow, check the *Birdhouse Sizing Guide*. The chickadee house, for example, needs a nesting area of only 4" x 4" x 8".

A note about all solid wood: try to use wood that is straight, and with as few knots as possible. This will make your job easier.

PLYWOOD

Plywood has a few major advantages over solid lumber:

- resistance to warping, swelling or shrinking

- strength

- resistance to splitting

- low cost

The only major drawback to plywood, especially thick plywood, is the difficulty in cutting and drilling. To do a good job with plywood, power tools help.

The best type of plywood to use for a birdhouse is exterior grade which is readily available, or marine grade which is a bit harder to find.

I prefer 1/4" plywood for roofing. Your cuts don't have to be perfect if you are covering the plywood with some kind of roofing material.

Just make sure the plywood you use has not been treated with any chemicals or finishes which could harm the occupants of the birdhouse. Copper-based "green" chemicals are not good for birds.

BASIC TOOLS

All of the birdhouses the *Architectural Replica Plans* section were built with hand tools — not very many of them — and minimum skill. This is all you need to be a successful birdhouse builder. As you gain a little experience, your projects will gain sophistication.

If you have power tools and you know how to use them, they can save you time and make your cuts a little more perfect.

If you have power tools but aren't sure how to use them, do not attempt to do so without first reading the manufacturer's instructions for the tool you want to use. Reading instructions followed by guidance from someone who is experienced with the power tool is the best way to learn. Remember, all blades and sharp objects can cut you if you're not careful. But powered, spinning blades are absolutely unforgiving of mistakes.

If you don't have power tools, not to worry. All of the hand tools you need to make a great birdhouse are shown below and listed on the next page.

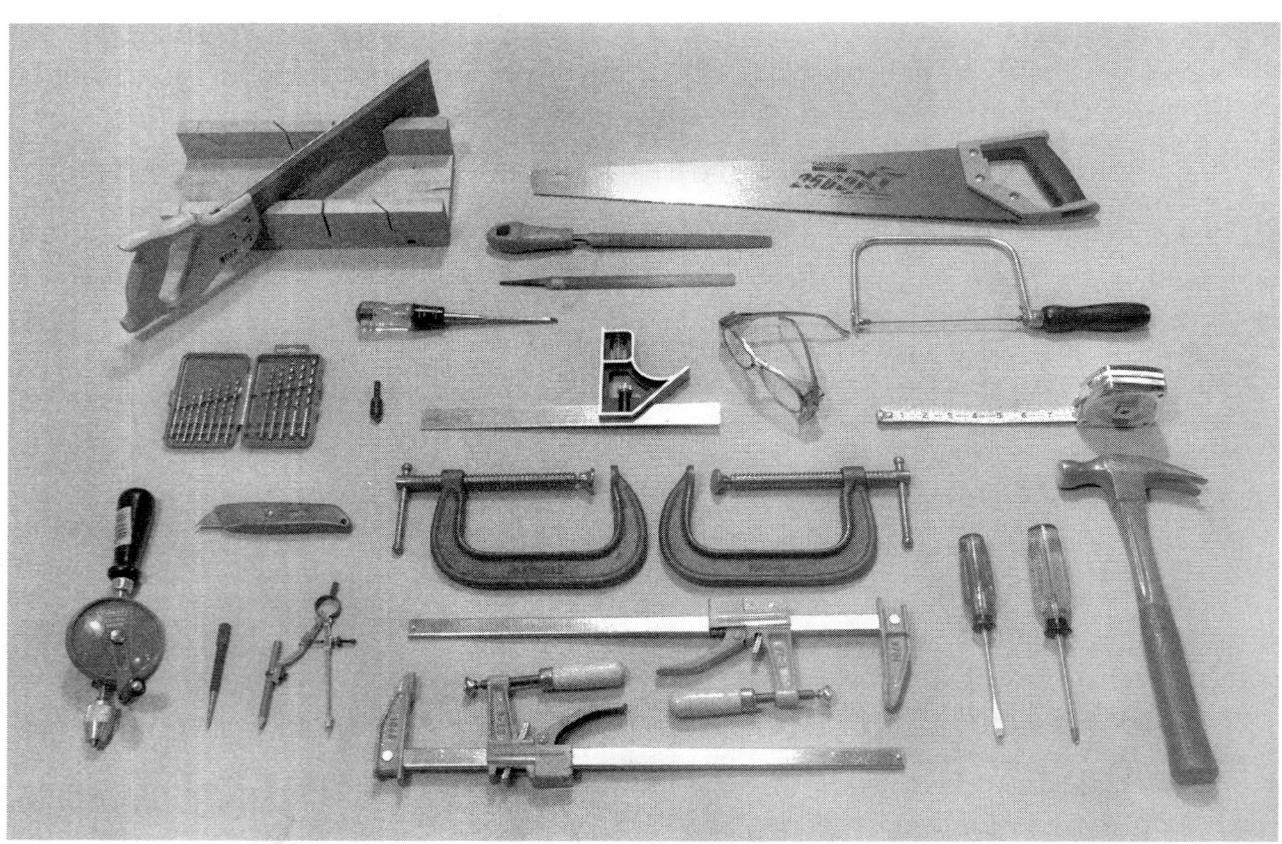

These are the tools I use to build birdhouses. They are all listed on the next page.

YOUR BASIC TOOL LIST:

- a good pair of safety goggles or safety glasses (I prefer the eyeglass type, with side protectors and polycarbonate lenses)
- a good universal saw for crosscutting and ripping
- a coping saw and plenty of replacement blades
- a backsaw and miter box (good to have, but not essential)
- a rasp file with flat and curved sides
- a half-round file
- a hammer
- screwdrivers — flat and Phillips
- 1/4" chisel
- 2 C-clamps
- 2 bar clamps
- a hand drill and assorted bits including a countersink bit
- a sanding block (this you can make out of scrap wood)
- a 2/32" nail set
- a combination square (good to have, but not essential)
- a ruler and pencil
- a utility knife
- a compass

The total price tag for all of this is about $160.00 for good quality tools. You can buy cheaper tools, but cheaper tools don't work as well or last as long. Tool buying is one area where you truly get what you pay for.

SOME NOTES ABOUT SAWS

Sawing is where you have the opportunity to turn a nice piece of lumber into a great birdhouse part, or a sanding block, depending on how well you work your saw. When buying saws, or evaluating the one you found in the basement, look for the following features:

- **Crosscut, ripsaw or universal.** Crosscut saws are for cutting across the grain of wood. Ripsaws are for cutting lengthwise with the grain. Universal saws are made to do both. When you find a saw, it should say what type it is on the side of the blade or on the packaging if it's a new saw. If it doesn't, look at the teeth by sighting lengthwise along the cutting edge and comparing what you see to the diagram. If the teeth bottoms are pointed, it is most likely a crosscut saw. If they are flat, it is most likely a ripsaw. If the teeth are a mixture of different styles, it is probably a universal saw which is fine for most woodworking needs.

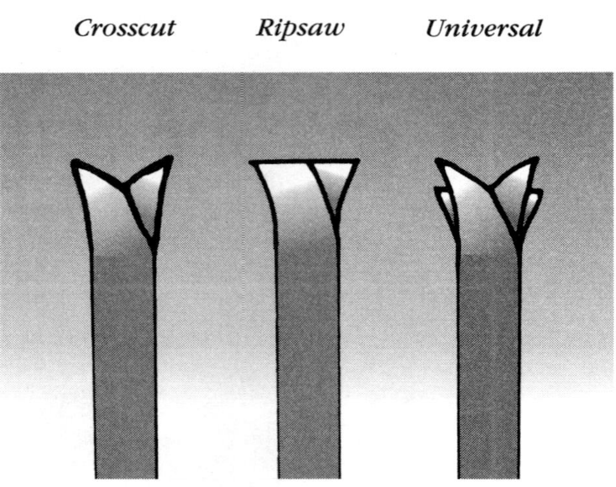

- **Coping saw.** You want your coping saw to be sturdy, with easily replaceable blades. If you buy a good name brand, you almost can't go wrong. But make sure the business end, the blade, is always sharp and straight. Always keep plenty of fresh blades on hand. Read the blade packages to make sure you are getting the right ones for your project.

- **Backsaw.** The backsaw has a solid "backbone" to keep it from bowing while you cut. It also has fine teeth. This combination makes the backsaw good for fine, straight cuts. When you use the backsaw with a miter box, you have the ability to make fine cuts at various angles. You can get by without the backsaw/miter box combination, but for the money, $7 for a wood miter box and $15 for a backsaw, it's a good investment.

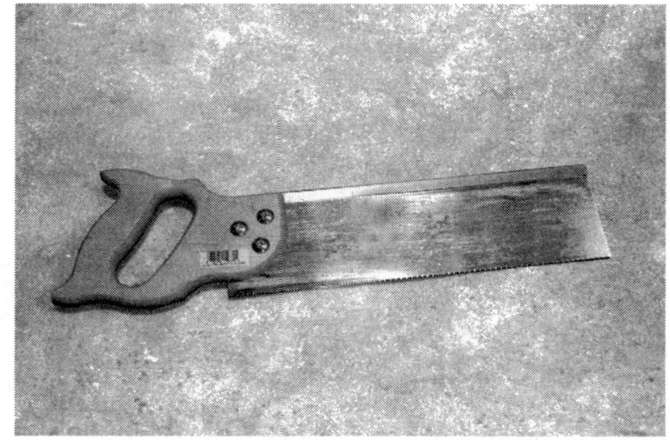

CAUTION

Safety is not just something to think about when you pick up a tool. It's also a state of mind which keeps you out of harm's way the whole time you're working. How do you work with a safety state of mind?

1. **Stay focused on the task at hand.** While woodworking is a great way to dissipate stress, it is not a mere distraction like watching TV. If something is bothering you to the extent that it takes up most of your brain, solve that problem before you pick up your woodworking tools.

2. **Know how to use your tools properly.** This means knowing how to position your materials, your tools and yourself securely, and at the best possible angles. Generally, if it doesn't feel right to you, it probably isn't right. Nothing is worse than losing control of your work in the middle of sawing, hammering, drilling or shaping. It can ruin both your project and your body. If you're not sure about the best way to work, look at a book about basic woodworking techniques. There are dozens of these books in print. You can find one in the library, the bookstore or at most home improvement centers.

3. **Keep your work area neat and uncluttered.** This is a simple practice that can really make a difference. Sawdust, small blocks of wood, loose nails and screws, paper and loose tools lying around are at best a distraction from the task at hand. At worst, they can trip you, slip you or cut you. Your work area will tend to get cluttered as you concentrate on the next thing you need to do. Just take a few minutes between tasks to tidy up. You'll think more clearly and your project will go together more easily.

4. **Always wear your safety glasses when working.** When you're in your wood shop, no matter how modest, you're in an industrial environment. Unlike your kitchen, living room or bedroom, there are eye hazards everywhere in your shop. Just because it's your basement or garage doesn't mean it's any less dangerous than a factory. One friend of mine was pulling a piece of wood from an overhead bin when a tiny flake of wood got in his eye: he was unable to work for the rest of the day. Another friend was driving a nail when a tiny piece of the nail flew into her eye: two days later an ophthalmologist removed the tiny rusting shard from her swollen eye. Get a good pair of comfortable safety glasses. Put them on before you begin your work and leave them there.

5. **Always read and follow the instructions, cautions and warnings that come with tools, paints and chemicals.**

6. **Keep your cutting tools sharp.** This includes saws, chisels, drill bits, files and utility knives. Dull tools can cause you to over exert, to force the tool instead of letting the tool do the work. Over exertion and forcing tools can lead to loss of control which can result in damage to your project or worse, injury to your body.

TECHNIQUES

This book is about doing whatever you're comfortable with now, and pushing yourself to new heights when it feels right to you.

If you're a beginner, you can use the tools and techniques in this book with good results. The more experienced birdhouse builder may use techniques (and some tools) not covered here. But don't try to do too much too soon. Experience is the best teacher. Start simple and work up to your masterpiece.

Depending on size and complexity, building a birdhouse can be a simple woodworking project that takes a few hours, or it can be an ongoing project that takes months to complete. It's up to you to decide which kind of project you're interested in working on.

If you've never worked on wood projects before, it is a good idea to get an inexpensive book on basic woodworking techniques. Mastering a new skill is always exciting.

Malcolm Wells calls this birdhouse his "Old Favorite."

FIVE THINGS YOU MUST KNOW

Before you begin designing or building a birdhouse, you for birds need to know five things which will ensure the safety of the birds you want to house.

Predator safeguards: Birds nesting in poorly designed or placed birdhouses can be easy pickings for predators. Sparrows, starlings, house wrens, cats, dogs, squirrels, raccoons, opossums and snakes all prey on nesting birds and their young. You can take some simple steps in birdhouse construction and placement to protect your birdhouse occupants. Some basic rules include:

- Proper box depth, roof and entrance hole design can discourage predators.

The block over the entrance hole helps keep furry little arms out of the nesting area.

- Adding a 3/4" block to the outside of the entrance hole keeps out the arms of raccoons, opossums and cats. If your design is an architecturally correct copy of a house with a chimney, consider putting the entry hole through the chimney where the wall thickness will be double.

- Adding a piece of sheet metal around the outside of the hole keeps squirrels from gnawing in.

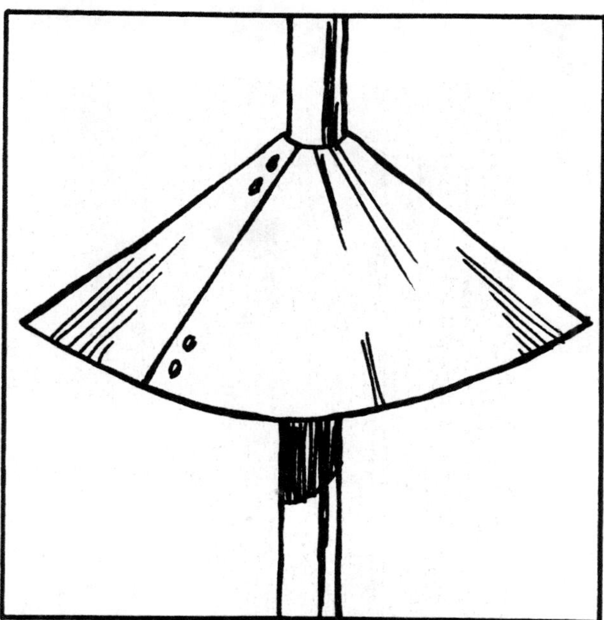

All post-mounted birdhouses should have a predator guard installed. Lots of climbing critters have a taste for birds and eggs.

- Mounting posts, especially wood, should have predator guards installed.

For more information, read the Protection from Predators section.

Entrance hole: This is one of the most important features a bird will be looking for. For size and placement of an entrance hole, follow the *Birdhouse Sizing Guide*.

Directly beneath the entrance hole, inside and outside, the surface should be rough to make it easier for the birds to get in and out of the house.

A classic bird stairway.

A gap between the wall and the roof provides good ventilation.

On the inside of a birdhouse made of smooth wood, you can make it easier for the birds if you put a 1/4" thick, 1/2" wide strip of rough wood diagonally beneath the hole. A piece of wire mesh mounted on the inside wall also works well.

On the outside of a smooth birdhouse, especially one that's painted, consider putting grooves or a small, thin cleat under the hole. You *do* want to give the occupants of the house a toe hold to use when entering the house. You *do not* want to make a perch on which predatory birds like starlings and house sparrows can loiter and wait for the occupants of the house to return.

NOTE: Perches made in the traditional way with dowels sticking out under the hole are dangerous invitations to predators.

Ventilation: Birdhouses can get extremely hot inside. Without proper ventilation, the birds inside can die on a hot day. There are several ways to provide ventilation. For single-family birdhouses, a 1/8" gap between the top of the side walls and the roof is adequate. There are numerous examples of this in the plans in this book. Another method is to drill 1/4" holes under the eaves of the roof. For multiple-family houses or houses with flat roofs, consider using a chimney. There's more about the chimney method in the *Advanced Building Techniques* section.

Drainage: It is almost certain that water will get in the birdhouse at some time or another. Well designed birdhouses with slanting, overhanging roofs may take in less water. But all birdhouses must have drainage holes in the floor. 1/8" holes in each corner and one in the center should be adequate. If you live in a rainy climate or have a birdhouse design that looks like it will take on water, make the holes 1/4" and consider cutting away the corners of the floor.

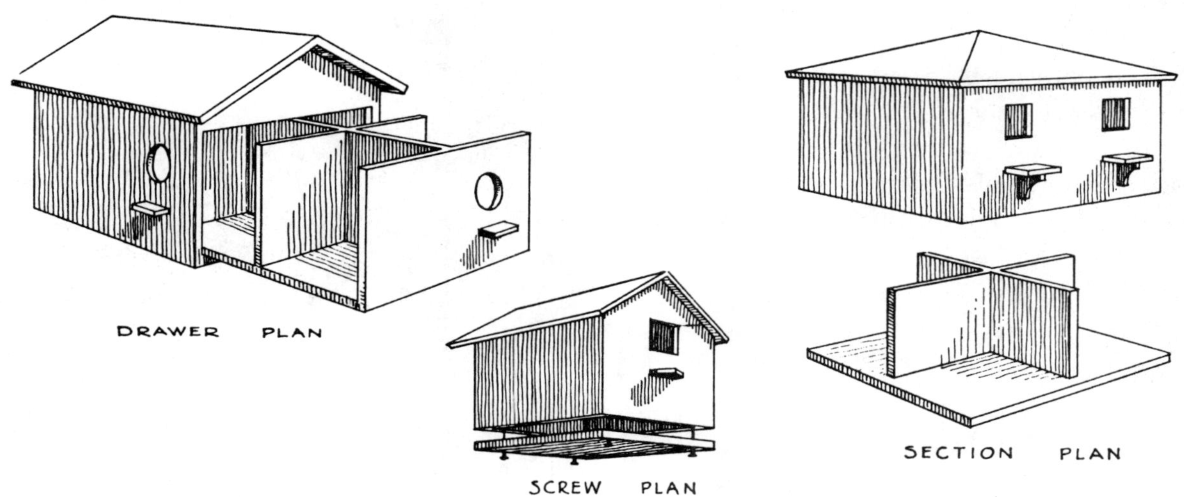

Cleaning access: Birdhouses must be cleaned thoroughly at the end of each nesting season. To clean the birdhouse, you need an easy way to open it up. Any flat part of a birdhouse can be used for access.

Typically, birdhouses have floors, roofs, sides, fronts or backs held in place with hinges, hooks or screws. Some birdhouses use drawers for the nesting area. For large purple martin houses with many apartments, exterior walls and roof can built as a single removable unit.

Depending on the design you choose for your birdhouse, one particular access technique will probably be more appropriate than others.

STRUCTURAL RECOMMENDATIONS

The birdhouses in the *Architectural Replica Plans* section follow the same basic time-tested structural techniques. You'll see the following techniques reflected in my plans, but you can do whatever makes sense for your project:

1. **Solid lumber.** Solid lumber for the main structural parts of the birdhouse gives it stability that will last through the ages if it's properly protected against water. Solid lumber is generally easier to work with than plywood. It's also easier to find useful scraps of solid wood, and it's easier to carry around in your car.

2. **Recessed floor.** When the floor is placed on the inside of the four walls, rain tends to run down the side of the house without wicking into the wood or running into the living area. There are no flat areas to hold puddles. Some houses need platforms for yards, shrubs, etc., but try to avoid mounting walls of the house on a flat platform if the house will be outside in a climate that receives average or greater rainfall.

A recessed floor.

Screws driven from the outside of the house to hold the floor in place

Hidden floor mounting using mending plates.

3. **Access to nesting area.** I prefer to use the floor of the birdhouse, even when it is post mounted. There are two ways to do this. The first is to simply hold the floor in place with screws driven in from the outside walls of the house. This is a strong floor attachment method, but it leaves screws visible from the outside of the house.

   The second floor attachment method is to use brass or brass-plated mending plates. This method is "hidden" and presents a neater appearance on the outside walls.

BUILDING BASICS

The best way to begin a project is to do first things first. On a birdhouse project, that means figuring out what you want to build. You can use the plans in this book, make your own plans using the methods described in the section *How To Turn Any Structure Into A Birdhouse,* or use plans you already have.

Once you have plans, you're ready to begin building. The following steps are generic, but they can keep you going in the right direction from start to finish on any birdhouse. These steps work well with the Architectural Replica plans I've included with this book. In the Architectural Replica plans, I've indicated where you need to deviate from these steps.

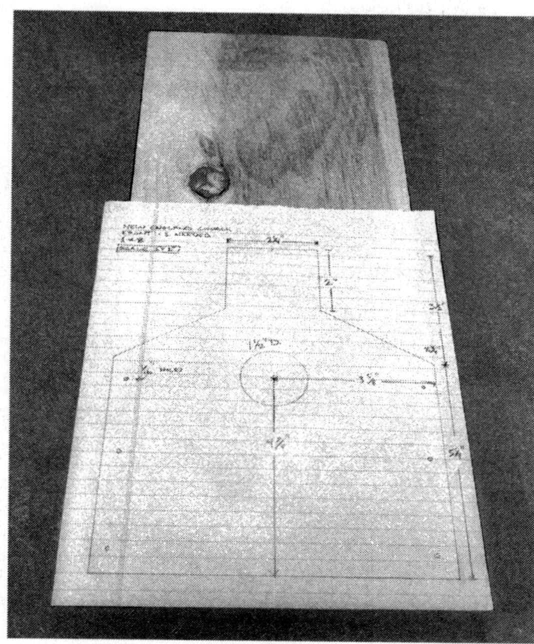

This is a full-scale plan for a bird-house part laid over the wood from which it will be cut. See item 1 below for an explanation.

1. TRANSFER YOUR PLANS TO YOUR WOOD.

If your plans are full scale, you can lay them on the lumber, align the straight edges with the factory edges on the lumber and use a sharp point to mark points of the plans through the paper to the lumber. An alternate method is to make copies of your full-scale plans, cut out the parts and use the cut outs as templates. You can also use a ruler and draw the parts on the lumber. It is a good idea to check your measurements twice. It's easy to read the wrong mark on a ruler and not notice it the first time around. One more note: factory edges are usually about as straight as you can get with wood (but check them to be sure). Use them for your straight edges wherever you can.

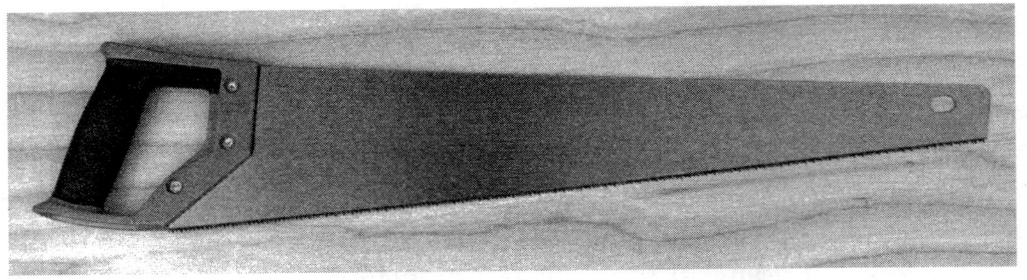

2. CUT OUT THE STRUCTURAL PARTS.

You can cut the trim pieces later. Sometimes you may be able to cut two duplicate parts at the same time. This is especially helpful for the end parts which have roof peaks. Cutting them at the same time lets you take care of the angle cutting once, and keep the angles the same on both pieces. When you're cutting straight lines, take your time and keep your saw straight. It's easier to cut straight than to straighten a crooked cut. If you need to cut a difficult angle (like a roof peak), try starting the cut with a small, easy to control saw. Then when you put your big saw to the task, it will be pointed in the right direction. And always saw outside of the line you made. In other words, leave the line on the piece you are making to use.

Dry clamping or taping the parts together before permanent assembly shows you if everything fits according to your plans.

3. SET UP THE PARTS IN RELATION TO WHERE THEY GO.

Use tape or clamps to hold things together if you need to. This step is to make sure everything goes together the way it's supposed to. When you're satisfied that you've done a good job cutting, take the structure apart and go on to the next step.

Drill a 1/4" hole inside the outline.

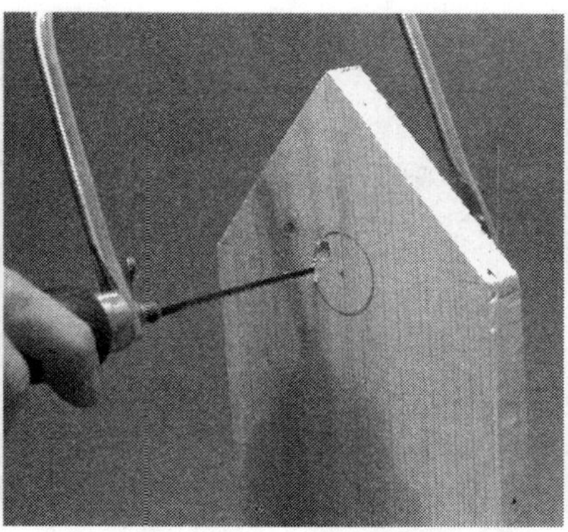

Cut along the outline with a coping saw.

Smooth the inside of the hole with a half-round file.

4. CUT THE ENTRANCE HOLE.

If you have not already marked the entrance hole, do so using the *Birdhouse Sizing Guidelines*. The center of the entrance hole should be measured from the floor of the interior, not the bottom of the exterior. If you're using 3/4" thick wood for a recessed floor, take that into account before cutting the hole. Use a compass to get a round outline for the hole. The hand-tool method to cut the hole is easier than it sounds. Drill a 1/4" hole just inside the edge of the outline. Pass a coping saw blade through the hole and attach it to the coping saw. Follow the outline with the saw. Use a round-faced file to smooth the inside of the hole. If you are using a power drill, you can use a spade bit or hole saw of the appropriate size. If you are using a power drill on plywood, you will need to use a hole saw. When you are finished, use your rasp to rough up the inside of the wall directly under the hole. Or you can glue a thin, rough strip of wood diagonally under the hole. This gives the birds more traction when getting out of the house.

5. FINISH YOUR CUT EDGES.

Here you will use a flat file for the real rough spots and a sanding block for the rest. Your goal is to make each edge as flat and smooth as possible for aesthetic and practical reasons. Aesthetically, flat, straight edges look better. Practically, they fit together better and provide more area for glue to bond with. But don't get carried away with your sanding. If you remove too much wood, it's pretty hard to put it back. Little gaps can be filled with exterior grade wood filler or spackle, or covered with trim.

Mending plates.

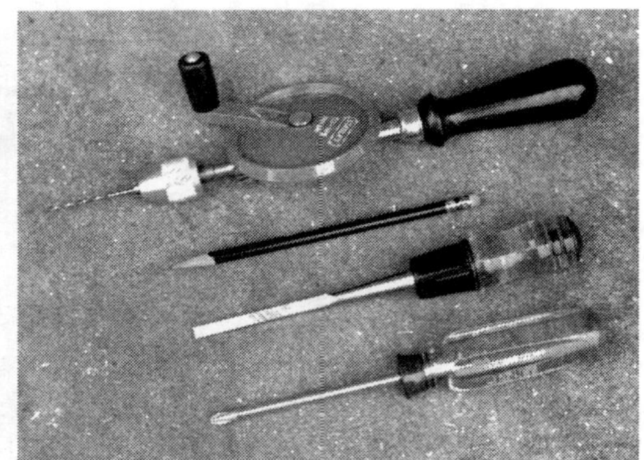

The tools you will need.

6. CUT CHANNELS FOR THE MENDING PLATES.

If you are using the Architectural Replica plans or will be using the mending-plate floor attachment method, you will want to cut channels in the bottoms of each side wall to accommodate the mending plates. Each channel should be 5/8" long, 9/16" wide and just a shade over 1/16" deep.

Use a pencil to outline the plate, about 5/8" in from the end of the wall. Put the edge of your chisel on the line, with the bevel edge toward the inside of the channel. Push or tap it into the wood to a depth of just over 1/16". Continue this until you have made depth cuts around each outline. With the bevel edge up, work from the inside of the wall toward the back of each channel, removing wood to make room for the mending plate. When most of the wood has been removed, finish the cut with the bevel edge of the chisel down. Place your mending plate in the channel. If it fits, mark where to drill the hole. Drill the hole. Repeat for the other mending plates.

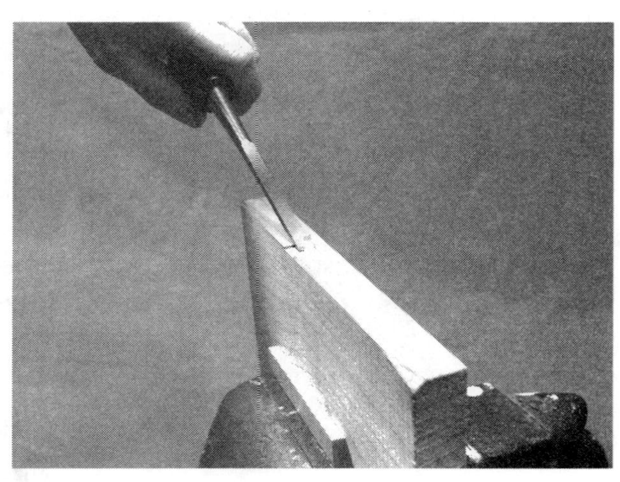

Cutting wood with a chisel can be rewarding but it takes some technique to do it properly. If you haven't used a chisel recently, practice on a piece of scrap wood. Be careful. Chisels are sharp and they can get away from you if you don't work them just right.

7. ASSEMBLE THE WALLS OF YOUR BIRDHOUSE.

Here you will be attaching the end walls (with roof peaks) to the side walls.

The nail method: Figure out where on the end walls you want the nails, and predrill a hole for each. Three nails for each wall — top, middle and bottom — works well. The holes should be just smaller than the nail you're using. (For a 4d galvanized finish nail that would be a 1/16" bit.) This keeps the wood from splitting and it makes it easier to hammer the nails into the wood. Hammer the nails through the ends until just a tiny portion of the tip sticks through the other side. Since you will be using a Type II wood glue at each joint, the nails are there primarily to hold the joint in place while the glue sets. Now you're ready to go. Brace the side wall in a vice, end facing up. If the vice is metal, place some thin wood between the jaws and your side wall to prevent marring. If you don't have a vice, use some clamps (use pads to prevent marring) and ingenuity, but make sure that when you start hammering, your work is not going to get away from you. Apply glue according to the manufacturer's instructions to the first joint you intend to make. Put the end wall in place, line up the edges and start hammering the nails. Wipe away any excess glue that squeezes out of the cracks. Repeat with the other side wall. You should now have an end wall with two side walls attached. Putting on the other end wall will be easier. Use your nailset to drive the heads of the nails below the surface of the wood. If you have bar clamps, clamp the structure together. Wipe away any glue that squeezes out of the joints. Let the glue set.

The screw method: Figure out where you want the screws. Drill a countersink for each, then a hole just smaller than the screw. If you have bar clamps, you can save time by clamping the structure together before you start drilling. Insert the screws through the end walls until the tips stick through the other side. Since you will be using a Type II wood glue at each joint, the screws are there primarily to hold the joint in place while the glue sets. Align the end wall with a side wall and press it together to mark where the screws will go. Do this with both ends and walls, keeping track of where each wall goes. Drill holes where the indentations from the screws appear on the ends of the walls. Apply glue to the first joint you intend to make, put the pieces together and tighten the screws until the heads are below the surface of the wood. Repeat until the structure is complete. If you have bar clamps, clamp the structure together. Wipe away any glue that squeezes out of the joints. Let the glue set.

8. TEMPORARILY ATTACH THE FLOOR.

To do this, you first put the floor in place inside the four walls. Holding the floor from the inside of the birdhouse, mark where to drill holes in the floor for the mending plate screws. Remove the floor. Drill holes in the floor. Replace the floor in the birdhouse. Attach the mending plates, which are attached to the walls, to the floor. Turn your birdhouse upright. Working down through the open roof, you will attach the inner partition (if necessary) and the floor stop blocks (if necessary). See steps 9 and 10.

9. ATTACH THE INNER PARTITION.

If your nesting area needs a partition to make it the right size, attach it using nails driven through holes (slightly smaller than the nails) drilled through the wall. Glue is not necessary as this part bears no structural load.

Partitions to make square nesting areas inside a rectangular box.

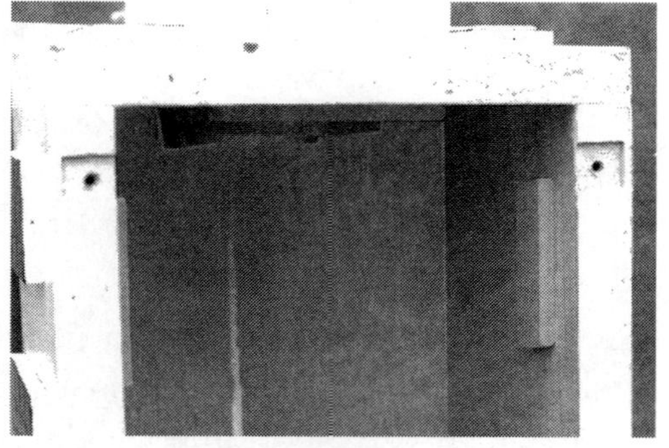

Floor stop blocks strengthen the floor for post mounting.

10. ATTACH FLOOR-STOP BLOCKS.

This is especially important if you are mounting your birdhouse on a post and you are using the floor as the removable access panel. Make your blocks about 3" long, 1/2" tall and 1/4" thick — lattice works quite well for this. Place one at each end and one on each side wall with the long flat side against the floor. If your house is a long rectangle, you might want to use two blocks on each side wall. Glue the floor stops in place using Type II wood glue. Be careful not to glue the stop blocks to the floor. Let the glue on the stop blocks set.

11. REMOVE THE FLOOR AND FLOOR ATTACHMENT HARDWARE.

12. TEMPORARILY ATTACH THE ROOF SECTIONS IN PLACE.

Use nails or strong tape. This will be helpful when you are cutting molding and trim. If you have no molding and trim, skip to step 15.

13. CUT ALL OF THE TRIM AND MOLDING YOU WILL BE USING.

This step lets the artist in you have some fun. It also lets you figure out ways to cover mistakes you can't fill in. To cut the ends of the molding, you will need a small miter tool. You can buy these at hobby and doll-house supply shops or you can make your own in 5 minutes. See the photo and description of the Homemade Mini Molding Miter. The goal is to join ends at a 45-degree angle. Once your pieces are cut, mark them for placement and set them aside for now.

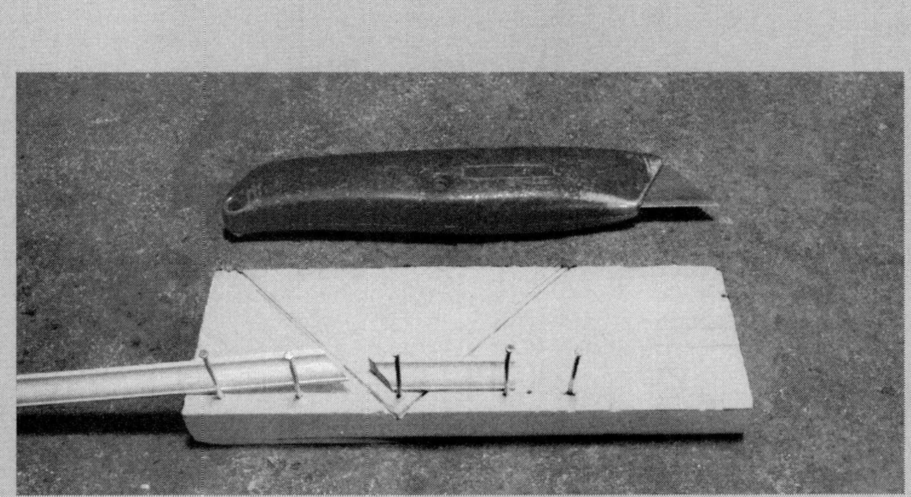

HOW TO MAKE AND USE A MINI MOLDING MITER

Find or make a scrap of wood about that's 2" x 6". Look for one that has that a factory edge along one of it's long sides. If it also has a factory edge on one of the ends, so much the better. Using a combination square or protractor, mark two 45-degree lines as shown. Place a row of nails 1/4" from the edge as shown, with one of the nails in the "V" formed by the angled lines. To use the Mini Molding Miter, place the molding along the nails, hold it tightly, and cut along one of the angles using your coping saw or utility knife.

14. REMOVE THE ROOF SECTIONS.

15. PRIME THE END GRAINS AND WALL TOPS.

Using exterior primer (if you are painting the birdhouse), coat the end grains that will support the roof, and the tops of the walls. When the primer is dry, follow with a coat of the paint you will be using for the rest of the house. Let it dry.

16. PERMANENTLY ATTACH THE ROOF.

Trim can be used to cover gaps between the walls and the roof, improving appearance and waterproofing. Trim can also be used to make architectural details like door and window frames.

17. ATTACH THE MOLDING, TRIM AND WOODEN DECORATIONS.

For the most part, you will glue trim pieces in place. If you need to hold them in place while the glue sets, use clamps or small brads to tack them until the glue sets. If your molding is too small to use brads, just use glue. If you do use brads, leave enough of the ends exposed so that you can pull them out when the glue is dry. If you have galvanized brads, you can leave them in the molding.

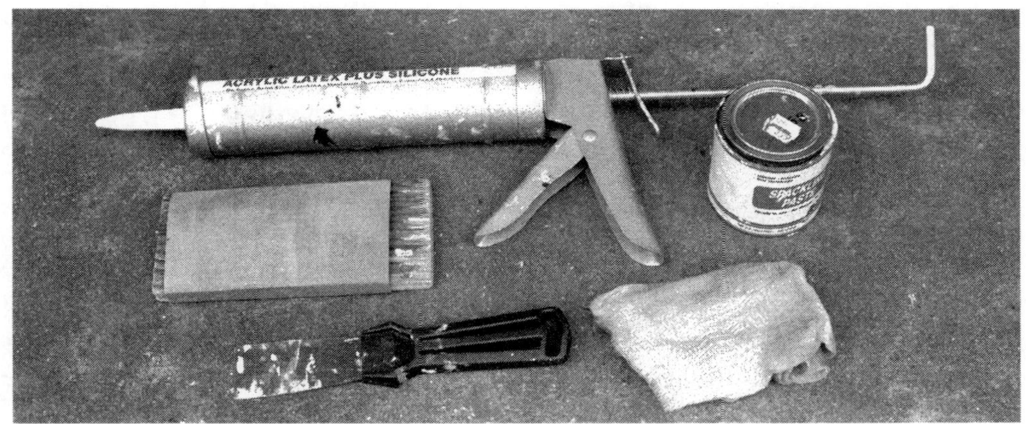

18. FILL ALL HOLES AND GAPS.

Use exterior grade wood filler or spackle (if you are going to paint).
Once the filler is dry, finish sand the birdhouse in preparation for painting. Use a tack cloth to remove dust before painting, finishing or giving
to a friend.

19. CAULK CRACKS AROUND THE ROOF WHICH COULD LEAK WATER.

20. DRILL DRAINAGE HOLES IN THE FLOOR.

One small hole in each corner and one in the center should be adequate.

21. ATTACH MOUNTING HARDWARE.

The best way to mount a birdhouse is from the bottom or back of the
birdhouse. Wren houses can be suspended. *(see Mounting Techniques
on page 45).*

22. PAINT OR FINISH THE HOUSE.

23. ATTACH THE FLOOR.

ADVANCED BUILDING TECHNIQUES

When you make birdhouses that look like peoplehouses, you will probably run into some architectural challenges. These include dormers, turrets, additions, intersecting rooflines, and chimney ventilation systems.

In most cases, these challenges can be solved easily. First, spend some time looking carefully at the architectural element you are trying to duplicate. Study it. When you understand the shape and structure, some ideas for birdhouse-sized solutions will come to mind.

As you become familiar with building materials and techniques, solutions will come to you even faster. Visits to well-stocked lumber yards, home centers, doll house supply stores and hobby shops will give you lots of good ideas.

Use your imagination. All building materials — wood, metal, plastics, fillers, roofing — are "plastic" and can be formed into countless shapes. If you know the properties of the material you are working with, you can make accurate decisions about what type of shape it will hold.

Experiment! When you've exhausted your imagination, work with your hands. Try different materials and tools until you hit on something that seems like it will work for your birdhouse.

Sometimes parts of a house that seem simple can challenge you. This back dormer seemed simple until I started to make plans based on it. It turned out to be a fairly complex mix of angles and dimensions.

DORMERS

If your birdhouse is small enough, you can make these out of solid wood. When you saw out your end walls, the waste pieces from the angles of the roof peaks are the right angle for your dormers. This can save you some time. (see Cape Cod plans)

If your dormers are bigger, you may have to build them from other materials. Lattice stripping is a good choice. It is very easy to work with and comes in several widths.

Dormers made from the angled lumber left after cutting the roof peaks.

TURRETS

Turrets come in two flavors. Segmented and round.

Either way, the turret you make will probably not be used as a structural element or living space. This frees you to use materials ranging from solid (like 4x4s) to delicate (like aluminum flashing).

The segmented turrets are fairly simple to construct. You can use just about any lumber that makes sense for the size of the turret.

Again, building with lattice is one good solution.

Round turrets can be made from large dowels for very small bird houses. For larger houses, PVC pipe is a good choice.

Putting a roof on a turret is requires a little imagination. In most cases, it is a cone of some sort. You can make a cone out of sheet metal, wood or a wood frame covered with roofing material or sheet metal.

ADDITIONS

Many houses will have more than one main structure. If the house has more than four corners, think of the smaller attached four-cornered structures as additions.

The easiest way to add them to your main birdhouse is to build them separately and attach them to the main structure. (See Green Mountain Ranch plans.)

When the additions are attached, they will either have their own separate roofs, or roofs which intersect with the main roof.

This birdhouse has an addition which is essentially a smaller birdhouse attached to the side.

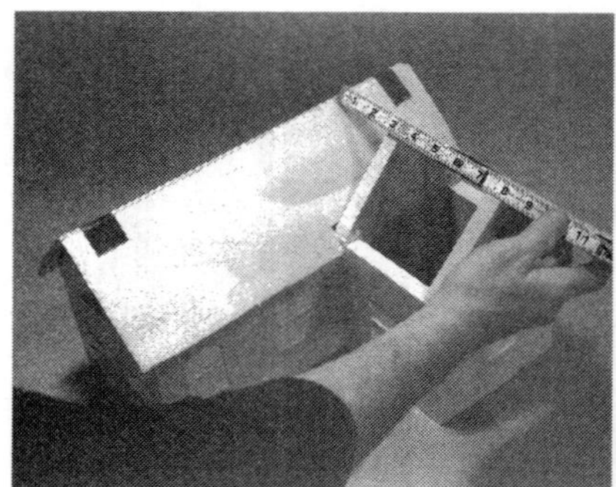

Measure how long you want the peak of the intersecting roof to be .

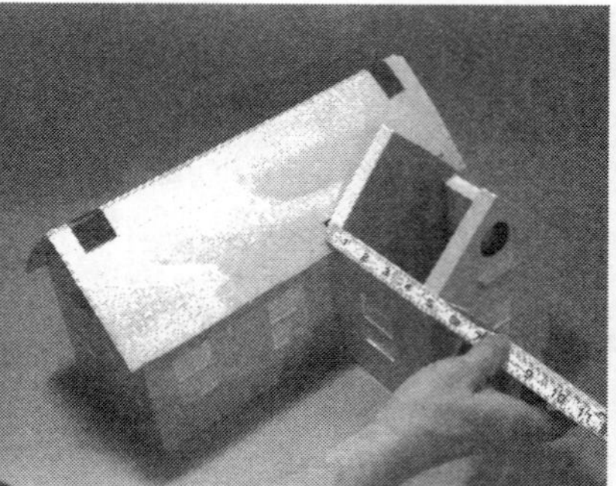

Measure from the bottom of the dominant roof. Transfer measurements to wood.

Make two pieces the same size and they should fit perfectly.

INTERSECTING ROOFLINES

The first thing you need to do is figure out which roofline is dominant. The dominant roof is the one that carries through from one end of the house to the other. It will have a gable at each end.

Cut roof underlayment to fit the dominant roof and put it in place. Next cut pieces long enough to span from the peak of the dominant roof to the proper wall overhang. To get the proper angle, measure how long the bottom edge of the roof needs to be to get from the base of the dominant roof to the overhang. (see Green Mountain Ranch plans)

CHIMNEY VENTILATION SYSTEMS

Chimneys can provide ventilation in birdhouses which might otherwise have ventilation problems due to design.

One example of this is a multiple family house which has a common ventilation shaft at the rear of the apartments which needs to be vented to the roof.

The chimney can be drilled out to create an air shaft to the outside. As long as it is constructed in a way that prevents water from getting inside, it should work well.

This two-inch tall chimney has four 1/4" holes to vent a flat roofed birdhouse. See Row House plans.

You must make sure the chimney has adequate air handling capacity. Air flow through a chimney can vary widely due to design.

All ventilation holes combined should equal 1 square inch of vent for every 18 square inches of floor space. This is an average measurement based on an average bird-house design. Upper apartments in multiple story houses will need more ventilation than lower story apartments. Thin roofed houses will need more ventilation to remove heat transferred through the roof.

IF IN DOUBT, ADD MORE VENTILATION. HEAT CAN KILL BIRDS AND THEIR EGGS.

ADVANCED WINDOWS AND DOORS

If you want to make your birdhouse a replica of a peoplehouse, you will probably want to give it some windows and doors.

The easiest way to do this is to simply paint them on, simply. Painting them on can also be the most difficult way, depending on how much realism you are trying for.

Most painted-on windows and doors will fall somewhere in the middle of the difficulty spectrum. It tends to be the little details — sash, curtain, color, hardware — that can make the painted-on things time consuming. (If you are an accomplished artist, painting may be the best route regardless of the complexity.)

Good painted-on windows and doors look real nice, but they're probably not as durable over the long run as wood or metal windows and doors.

Doors and windows made of wood can be carved into the structure or added on to it.

These recessed windows and door were carved into the wood with a chisel. If you want to get real fancy, you can saw out the window entirely and put in panes of glass — not recommended for functional birdhouses. Birds prefer privacy.

Add-on windows made from lattice strips look quite good and are a bit easier to make than the recessed windows. You can also make add-on windows using thin strips of molding for frames, sills and sashes.

Wood windows and doors provides a measure of permanency paint cannot match. Permanency is a requirement if you want your functional birdhouse to be 1) a collectible, 2) an heirloom, and 3) an antique someday.

Paint can, over the years, peel, fade, blister and generally wash away. It's possible that the windows and doors that look great painted on today may be barely visible after a number of seasons in the elements.

Wood doors and windows will be there, in some form, years from now. By using wood, you can be sure that at least the size, shape and location of doors and windows will be there for posterity.

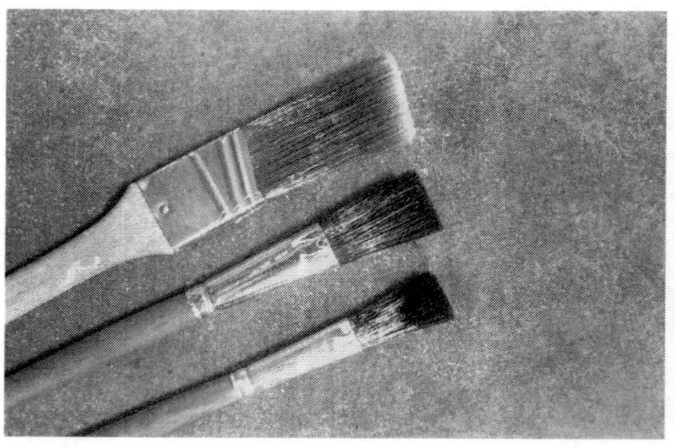 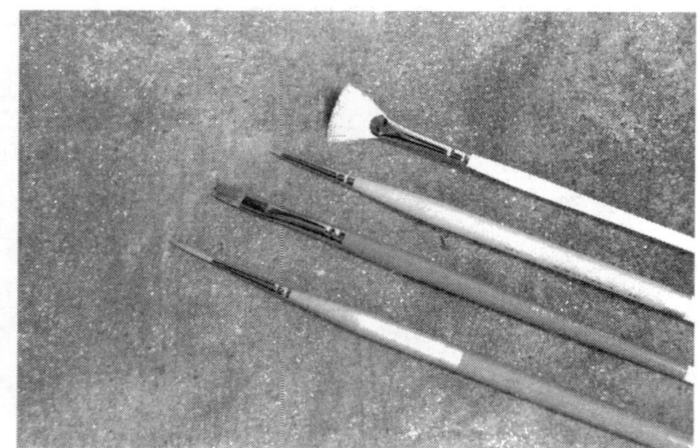

PAINTING AND STAINING

This operation is pretty straightforward. There are just two basic rules:

- Leave the inside of the birdhouse unfinished. Paints and finishes inside the birdhouse can make your guests sick.

- If the birdhouse is destined for the great outdoors, use good quality exterior finishes. Oil based and latex paints both work well. For a natural finish, use an oil stain or polyurethane. Many higher quality woods weather well without any finish at all. Inexpensive woods fare better with a good coat of paint. Using exterior primer under the paint makes it more durable.

LATEX VERSUS OIL PAINT

The latest latex paints are, arguably, as durable as oil paints. The major benefit to using latex paint is that it can be thinned and cleaned up with water instead of harsh chemicals.

The only drawback is that latex paint sets real fast. This means you have to work real fast, and get it right pretty much on the first pass.

Touching up a painted surface after the paint has started to set can result in unsightly brush marks.

THINNING YOUR PAINT

You can buy a little extra time to fix mistakes by thinning your latex paint.

Thinning will also greatly reduce the appearance of brush strokes.

Follow the manufacturer's instructions for thinning if there are any. Many manufacturers don't recommend thinning their exterior latex paint. They probably think you're painting a people house, not a birdhouse.

If there aren't instructions on how to thin the paint, experiment.

Add small amounts of water to a small amount of the paint.

Apply the mixture to a primed piece of wood that is lying flat.

When the paint is just thin enough that brush strokes "melt" after it is applied, it is ready.

Always experiment with thinned paint before you apply it to your masterpiece!

A birdhouse that looks like a hungry cat or raptor might send the wrong message.

COLORS

The colors birds prefer are the natural ones: soft tans, grays, browns and greens. Purple martins also like white paint. But if your artistic instincts overrule your naturalistic instincts, go ahead and make your birdhouse any color you want. Some birds may have offbeat tastes and like your creation, regardless of the color.

Just try to keep it from looking too scary. Birds do get upset by patterns and colors that remind them of predators.

MOUNTING TECHNIQUES

There are three basic ways to mount a birdhouse.

- post mounted

- back mounted

- suspended

Of the three, post and back mounted are the sturdiest. Suspended birdhouses swing in the wind, a ride most birds will not tolerate (Wrens don't seem to mind).

To post mount a birdhouse, use 4" x 4" pressure treated stock with a 3/4" thick block at the top. The block should be sized so that it is slightly smaller than the width of the floor. To mount the house to this, place 1-1/4" brass screws in each corner of the block.

You can also use 3/4" galvanized steel pipe to mount a birdhouse. A female floor flange should be mounted to the birdhouse.

Make sure when you are putting screws in the bottom of the house that the ends don't protrude into the nesting area.

To back mount, place a 1" x 4" board at the back of the house. You want to make the board long enough so that you have about four inches top, bottom, or top and bottom to nail into.

HOW TO TURN ANY STRUCTURE INTO A BIRDHOUSE

Probably the most rewarding birdhouse project is the one that is based on your design. It is not only a birdhouse, it is a vision of yours turned into a solid three-dimensional object. There are three basic ways to develop your own plans, and each way will bring you satisfaction and a lot of fun.

In practice you will probably combine more than one of these methods to arrive at your design. Don't fret, it will come naturally to you as you try it.

Reckoning with a ruler is a fast, accurate way to get the dimensions of a building.

Once you have the dimensions, transfer them to your rough sketch.

The "Reckoning" Method: This is the most accurate way to make plans for a copy of a real building.

You'll need a 12" ruler, a pad of paper and a pencil. Position yourself a short distance away from the building (25 - 75 feet), facing one side squarely. Make a rough sketch of that side of the building. Don't worry about getting proportions right, you'll do that later.

Next, hold your ruler at arm's length, toward the building. Close one eye and sight down your arm with the other. Line up the end of the ruler with the edge of the building, then read the inch mark that is lined up with the other edge of the building. Note on your sketch how many "inches" wide the building is. Do the same with height, rooflines, chimneys, windows, doors, and all major architectural elements.

Repeat this procedure for all four sides of the building, if possible. As you move around the building, try to stay the same distance away. To figure out if you're the same distance away, just use your ruler. If the building was 8 "inches" high in your first measurement, and it is the same height now that you have moved, you're the right distance away. If it is impossible to get the same distance away, estimate best you can based on other measurements you have taken. Windows, doors and the height of the roofline as measured in your first measurement can be a good guide.

You'll find that most major parts of a house are often the same all around a house — walls, rooflines, windows, and doors. If you only measure what you have to and estimate the rest, you'll save time.

When you've gotten all of the measurements you need, skip ahead to the section called *Making Plans.*

The "Snapshot" Method: This is a good way to copy a real building using a picture you took while on vacation, or one you found in a shoe box in your aunt's desk drawer. It's also a good method to use if you see a building you want to "birdhouse" but aren't able stand around using the reckoning method.

First, you just take a picture of each of the building's sides. If you can't do that, get what you can, and keep in mind, just one picture will do. Your memory can fill in the missing details. Also keep in mind that you don't need a camera at all. Just make a sketch while it's still fresh in your mind, and use the "Mind's Eye" method to finish your design.

Next, you'll need your snapshot (or sketch), a ruler, a pencil and a pad of paper.

Now take the big measurements — length, width, height. Because your snapshot will probably have some perspective and lens distortion in it, your measurements are going to be approximate. That's okay. Your real task here is to record the basic shape and proportions of the building.

Beware: sometimes camera lenses and perspective can really distort the relationship between width and depth. If your main structural measurements don't feel right to you, draw a floor plan based on them. If it looks wrong, adjust your measurements until it looks right.

When you have the building sketched and measured, go back and measure windows, doors, etc., and placements of these elements.

All done? Skip ahead to the *Making Plans* section.

Camera lenses often distort shapes and sizes. If your building has windows the same size, measure them all and come up with an average.

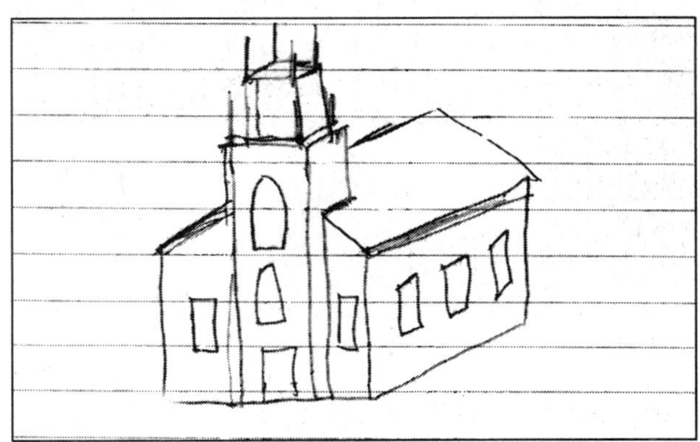

This is how I began making the New England Church plans using the Mind's Eye method.

The "Mind's Eye" Method: This is what you're going to use if most or all of your design is in your head. Here you're free to do just about whatever you want. Sounds pretty scary. It's not really. Just start with any type of structure in mind, and make a sketch. *Don't get discouraged if your first sketches don't look like what you're thinking about. Use what you learn making one sketch to make the next version better.* You'll be surprised at how quickly your vision comes alive on paper.

Once you've got a sketch you're happy with, you need to size it. You can put in approximate measurements if any come to you at this stage, or you can start making plans for your dream birdhouse.

MAKING PLANS

Now that you have a sketch worked out, it's time to push your vision a little closer to reality. This is where you get to see what the final shape is going to look like. If you make full-scale plans, you'll also see how big it will be.

By the way, if you haven't read the *Materials, Tools and Techniques* section, you should do so before making plans. At least read over the *Techniques* section. It will help you visualize how the parts go together.

The plans described in this section are for birdhouses which are functional (from a bird's point of view, that is) or both decorative and functional. Remember, if your birdhouse will reside inside your peoplehouse (just decorative), you can be a lot freer with the building techniques and materials you use.

If you look at the plans in this book, you'll begin to see some similarities in each project. Borrow building techniques from these plans wherever you can. It will save you time and the results should be good.

A WORD OR TWO BEFORE YOU START

There are two types of plans you can make:

1. Reduced scale. These plans are necessary when your parts are going to be too big to fit on normal paper, or if you just want to draw all of your parts on one sheet to save paper. These plans are suited to the more experienced builder who is less likely to make a mistake in sizing the parts of the birdhouse.

2. Full scale. With these plans, your drawings become patterns which you can transfer to your wood. To save time and paper, you can draw directly on the wood, but paper plans are nice to have as a record of your design. Full scale plans are handy for smaller birdhouses that have parts which will fit on regular 8-1/2" x 11" paper. If you want to make full scale plans and your parts are too big, you can always use bigger paper or tape small sheets together. Making full scale plans also relieves you of proportionally reducing your parts to fit on a single page. As an added benefit, with full scale plans, you can see more clearly if you've made a sizing mistake — everything's real size.

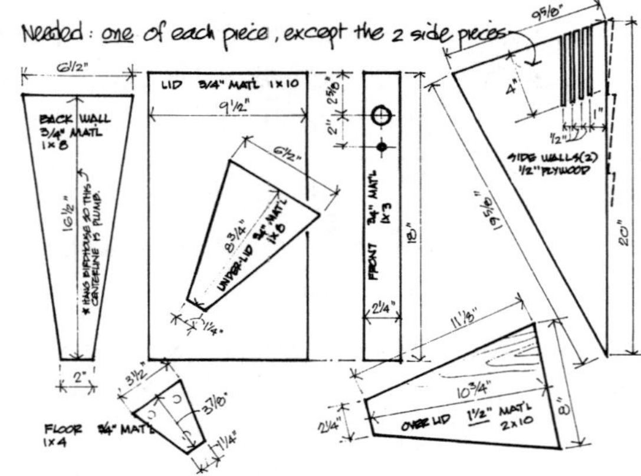

Reduced scale plans.

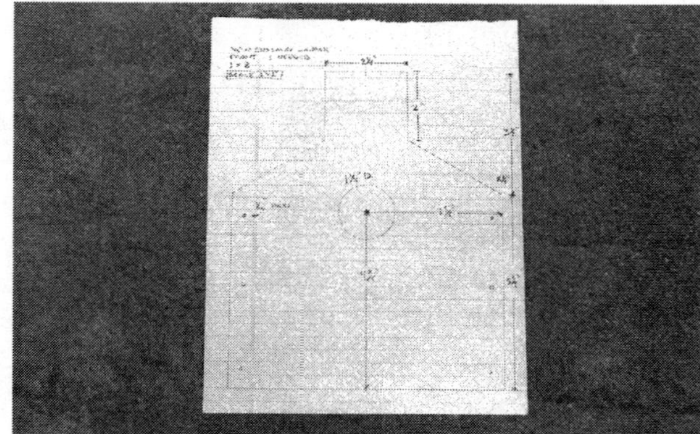

Full scale plans.

Whether you're making reduced or full scale plans, you need to put the Builder in you to work for a while and get the technical stuff worked out before you start cutting up your lumber.

To make your plans, you're going to need your trusty 12" ruler, a pencil, some paper (I prefer lined or graph to help line things up), and tape if you need to make big plans.

Measure your boards to give you a sense of how to size your birdhouse. Then refer to the Birdhouse Sizing Guide.

SOME QUESTIONS YOU NEED TO ANSWER

Before you get started, you need to juggle some information for a few minutes to decide on the best size for your birdhouse.

What is the basic shape of your structure? And what type of bird could live in the nesting areas provided by your birdhouse? To answer these questions, think about the floor plan and the height. Is your floor plan square or rectangular? Is the structure taller than it is wide? Check the *Birdhouse Sizing Guide* for nesting area dimensions that look close to the shape of your structure. It doesn't have to be perfect, and you can make a small square nesting area inside a big rectangular structure by using a partition. (You'll see some of these in my plans.) Keep in mind, though, the height of the nesting area is important.

How much building material do you have? Can you get all of the parts you need from a board you have, or do you need to buy a wider one, or use plywood? The most convenient way to go is to scale your birdhouse so that the widest part of your end pieces span the width of your board

Now that you have an idea of how big to make your birdhouse, you're ready to start figuring and drawing.

THE MATH PART

It's not as bad as it sounds. In fact, once you come up with your Magic Number, the rest just flows. After you work through this procedure once, it will come naturally to you when you do it again.

The Magic Number is what you will multiply all of your sketch dimensions by to get your plan dimensions.

In the example illustrated on the next page, (I used the snapshot method to make my sketch), I figured that my sketch floor plan looked right at 1-1/2" x 2".

Next, I figured that the house shape would make a good warbler house — roughly 5" x 5" x 6". So I need the smallest internal dimension to be 5". Smallest equals shortest side of the structure, in this case, the end of the house.

Important: Since the board I'm using is a 1x8, which is actually 7-1/4" wide, that is as wide as I want to go with the ends of the house. If I subtract 1-1/2" from that to allow for the other walls, I'm left with an internal dimension of 5-3/4". Close enough for warblers. So my birdhouse will be 7-1/4" wide.

This is what I had in mind when I made the calculations on the next page.

THE MAGIC NUMBER: I need to convert 1-1/2" (the shortest side on my sketch) to 7-1/4". I divide 7.25 (7-1/4") by 1.5 (1-1/2") to get approximately 4.8. If I multiply all of my other sketch dimensions by the magic number 4.8, the house gets enlarged while keeping its shape. It makes it easier if you round off your figures to the nearest quarter inch. For your calculations,

$$1/8" = 0.125$$
$$1/4" = 0.25$$
$$3/8" = 0.375$$
$$1/2" = 0.5$$
$$5/8" = 0.625$$
$$3/4" = 0.75$$
$$7/8" = 0.875$$
$$1" = 1.0$$

2-1/8" tall on the sketch becomes 10.2" which rounds off to 10-1/4" tall on the plan

2" width on the sketch becomes 9.6" which rounds off to 9-1/2". Since these walls are going inside the end walls, we'll subtract 1-1/2" (3/4" end-wall thickness x 2) from the 9-1/2" to get 8".

The floor will be 5-3/4" x 8".

Now, draw a scaled-up sketch like the illustration on the next page.

This is the point where you have to figure out how all the parts are going to go together. The *Basic Structural Guidelines* on page 52 might help.

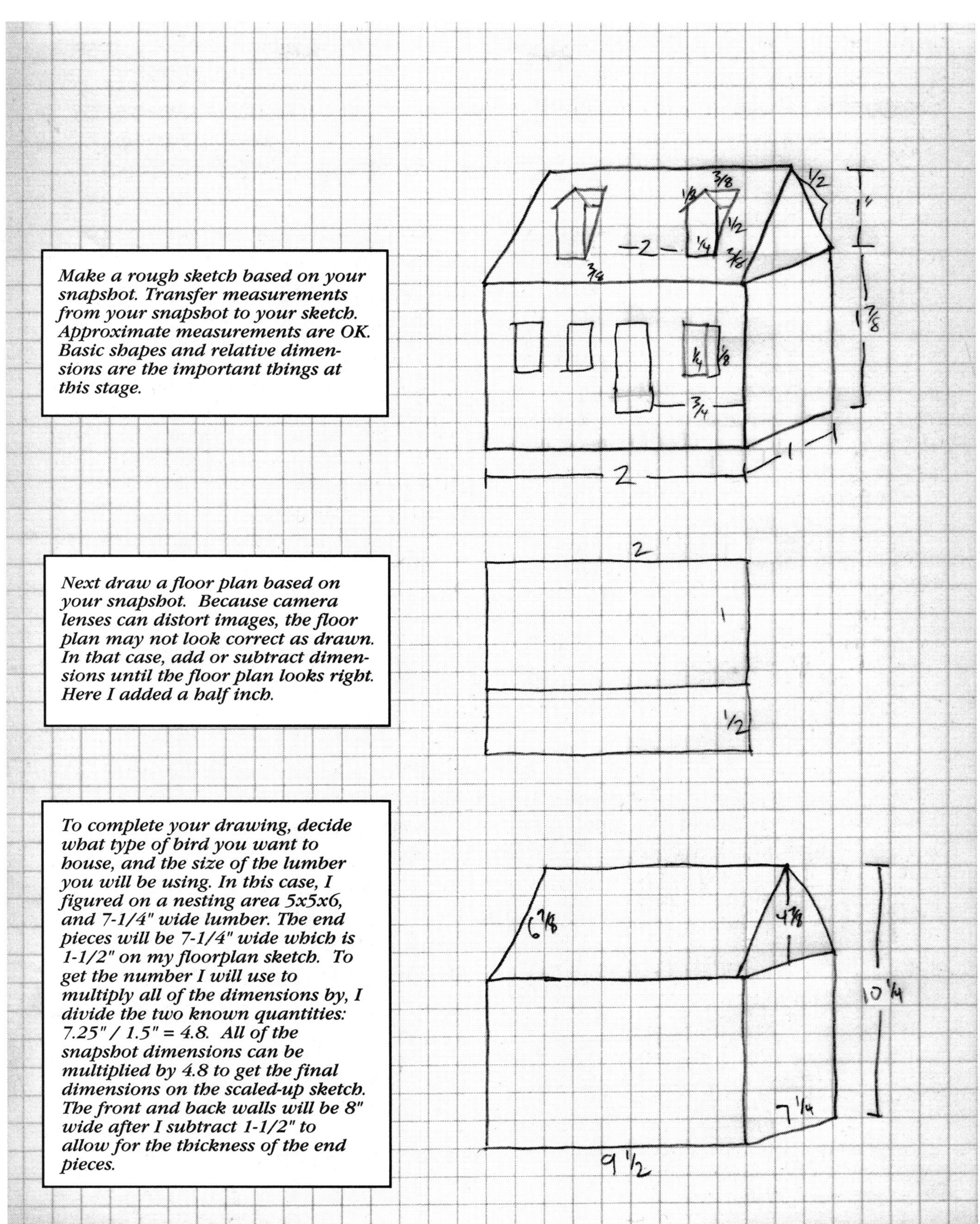

Make a rough sketch based on your snapshot. Transfer measurements from your snapshot to your sketch. Approximate measurements are OK. Basic shapes and relative dimensions are the important things at this stage.

Next draw a floor plan based on your snapshot. Because camera lenses can distort images, the floor plan may not look correct as drawn. In that case, add or subtract dimensions until the floor plan looks right. Here I added a half inch.

To complete your drawing, decide what type of bird you want to house, and the size of the lumber you will be using. In this case, I figured on a nesting area 5x5x6, and 7-1/4" wide lumber. The end pieces will be 7-1/4" wide which is 1-1/2" on my floorplan sketch. To get the number I will use to multiply all of the dimensions by, I divide the two known quantities: 7.25" / 1.5" = 4.8. All of the snapshot dimensions can be multiplied by 4.8 to get the final dimensions on the scaled-up sketch. The front and back walls will be 8" wide after I subtract 1-1/2" to allow for the thickness of the end pieces.

BASIC STRUCTURAL GUIDELINES (TO HELP IN MAKING PLANS)

1. The width of the end walls (the ones with the roof peaks) should be the outside dimension of the house. That means the other walls (the ones under the eaves of the roof) go inside. This makes it easier to install the roof.

2. The walls that are under the eaves of the roof should be about 1/8" shorter than the shoulder of the end walls for ventilation. If you have a flat roof that is tilted, make the wall under the low side a bit shorter than the walls supporting the roof. The ventilation opening should always be protected by the eaves of the roof to keep rain out. An alternate method of ventilation is to drill 1/4" holes near the top of the house in an area that is protected from the rain. Ventilation can also be accomplished by using a chimney vent. *(see Advanced Building Techniques)*

3. Figure out where the entry hole needs to be and mark it.

4. The floor needs to have drainage holes in case water gets in. One 1/8" hole in each corner and one in the center is adequate.

5. One of your flat surfaces needs to open so you can clean the inside of the nesting area each year. I recommend installing the recessed floor with brass mending plates or screws.

6. The roof itself can be made of any material that is waterproof or can be made waterproof — plywood, solid lumber, sheet metal, roofing material and more. In the Cape Cod project, I needed to mount dormer windows on the roof so I used plywood.

7. Chimneys, doors and porches, windows, decoration, and trim are the last things to plan. Since these are not structural elements, you can use your imagination in putting these together. Windows, doors, decoration and trim can often be painted on.

By now, you should have a good idea of what your birdhouse will look like full scale. If you run into any questions about how you should assemble your structure, just refer to the completed plans in this book for guidelines.

Once you get your basic structure built — the four (or more) walls and roof, the rest will come pretty easily.

STUMPED?

Some people have the ability to look at a three-dimensional object and instantly know how all of the parts go together. Other people can look at flat plans and "see" what the three-dimensional object will look like.

Most of us, however, struggle with this kind of stuff.

If you have come across a part of your plans that you just can't work out on paper, try cardboard.

Cardboard lets you work in three dimensions and see how parts go together. I had to resort to this technique to make the dormers for the Cape Cod plans. Just remember: the wood you will be working with is a lot thicker than cardboard. Allow for this in your measurements, and put the cardboard parts together exactly as the wood parts go together.

In cardboard, you can try all the variations you can think of. You'll be surprised at how quickly working in cardboard can show you what you couldn't see on paper.

Hunt, gather, or make an architecturally correct birdhouse?

This is the cardboard version of the Cape Cod. It was here that the back and front dormers first sprung off the page and into life.

This is what it looked like after I traced the cardboard dormer templates onto wood and started building.

READY TO USE PLANS

This section has three groups of plans:

The plans immediately following this page are designs I made especially for this book. They are, for the most part, accurate copies of real human dwellings.

The plans beginning on page 107 are by architect Malcolm Wells, who primarily designs underground peoplehouses. His birdhouses and feeders are great looking and, unlike 99.9% of peoplehouses, blend well with their environments.

The plans beginning on page 117 are by Gladstone Califf, a woodworking instructor who wrote a comprehensive (for its time) book about birdhouses in 1924. Mr. Califf's plans include some interesting designs, but you may want to update them to reflect current birdhouse technology. You will find information about current birdhouse technology in the *Techniques* section of this book.

ARCHITECTURAL REPLICA PLANS

A drive through the New England countryside can overwhelm your senses with the beauty and simplicity of it all. Tucked away in almost every little village, you'll probably find a church that looks something like this one. This design was bagged using a combination of "snapshot" and "mind's eye" methods.

It is designed for swallows, with a nesting area 5-3/4" square and 6" deep. You can make it bigger or smaller, or change it to look like your favorite place of worship.

  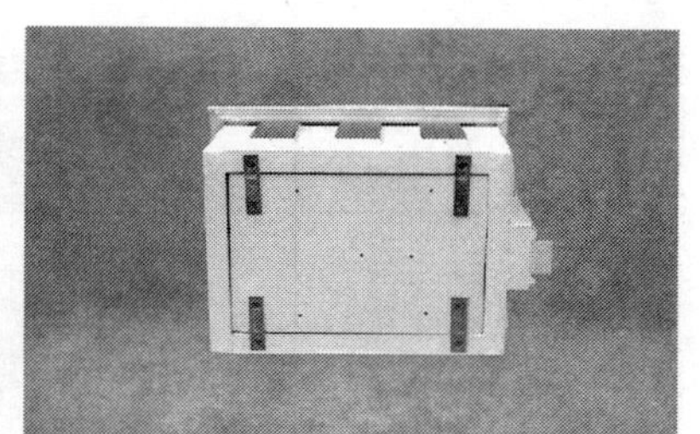

Materials list:

(2) 3-foot 1 x 8 boards

2-1/2 square feet of 1/4" or thinner plywood

(10) 2-1/2" doll house balusters (8 needed, 2 extra in case you break one or two)

4 feet of doll house trim (see photo for suggestions)

Assorted 1/4" and 1/2" moldings (see photo for suggestions)

(1) roofing shingle

4d galvanized finish nails

4d galvanized common nails (to attach roof)

3/4" 18 ga. brads (preferably galvanized)

7/16" aluminum or copper tacks (to attach roof shingle)

Type II weatherproof wood glue

(4) brass mending plates with brass screws

Latex waterproof caulk

Exterior primer and paint

Instructions:

All parts in the following plans are full scale *except* the roof parts. The roof parts are 1/2 scale.

For instructions on how this birdhouse is built, refer to the Building Basics section.

What is not covered in Building Basics is the assembly of the steeple and bell tower.

Steeple instructions:

1. Cut front and back steeple pieces.

2. Cut entrance hole in front steeple piece.

3. Cut entrance hole in front of church in same position as hole on front steeple piece.

4. Glue and clamp front steeple piece to front of church.

5. Glue and clamp back steeple piece to back of front of church.

Bell tower instructions:

1. Glue the two pieces of 3/4" stock together to make the belfry.

2. Drive brads through the underside of both platforms, one brad in each corner, 1/8" in from corner. These will hold your balusters in place.

3. Cut 4 of the balusters a bit shorter than the other four. These will go on the top platform. Carefully sand the bottoms of all 8 balusters flat (doll house balusters are not always flat on the bottom.)

4. Place a brad in your hand drill (use a bit if you have one just smaller than the brads you are using). Brace each baluster, bottom end up. Drill a hole into the base of each baluster, deep enough for complete insertion of the brads on the platforms.

5. Place a tiny drop of glue at the top of a brad that is sticking up through the platform. "Screw" the baluster down until its base contacts the platform. Square it up with the platform, and get it as perpendicular to the platform as possible. Wipe away excess glue. Repeat with the other seven balusters. Let glue dry.

6. Cut trim to go between balusters. Glue in place. Wipe away excess glue. Let glue dry.

7. Cut and attach molding around top of belfry. Let glue dry.

8. Cut and attach molding around top of bell tower on church. Let glue dry.

9. Glue top platform to belfry. Clamp, let glue dry.

10. Glue bottom platform to top of bell tower on church. Clamp, let glue dry.

11. Glue belfry assembly to bottom plat form. Clamp, let glue dry.

12. Carefully prime and paint. You might want to try dipping this whole assembly in a can of paint. BE CAREFUL! Most primers and paints as they come right out of the can are way too thick for dipping. IF THE PAINT IS TOO THICK AND YOU DIP, YOU'LL RUIN YOUR WORK! EXPERIMENT with similar wooden parts and thinned paint before committing your belfry to a dip. If you're not feeling adventurous, you can apply primer and paint with a brush. Be careful, though, the parts are delicate. You could also spray the assembly, but spraying paint tends to destroy the atmosphere, and regardless of how easy it looks on TV, spraying paint is no day at the beach.

The door and window are roughly actual size.

NEW ENGLAND CHURCH

FRONT
1 NEEDED
1 X 8

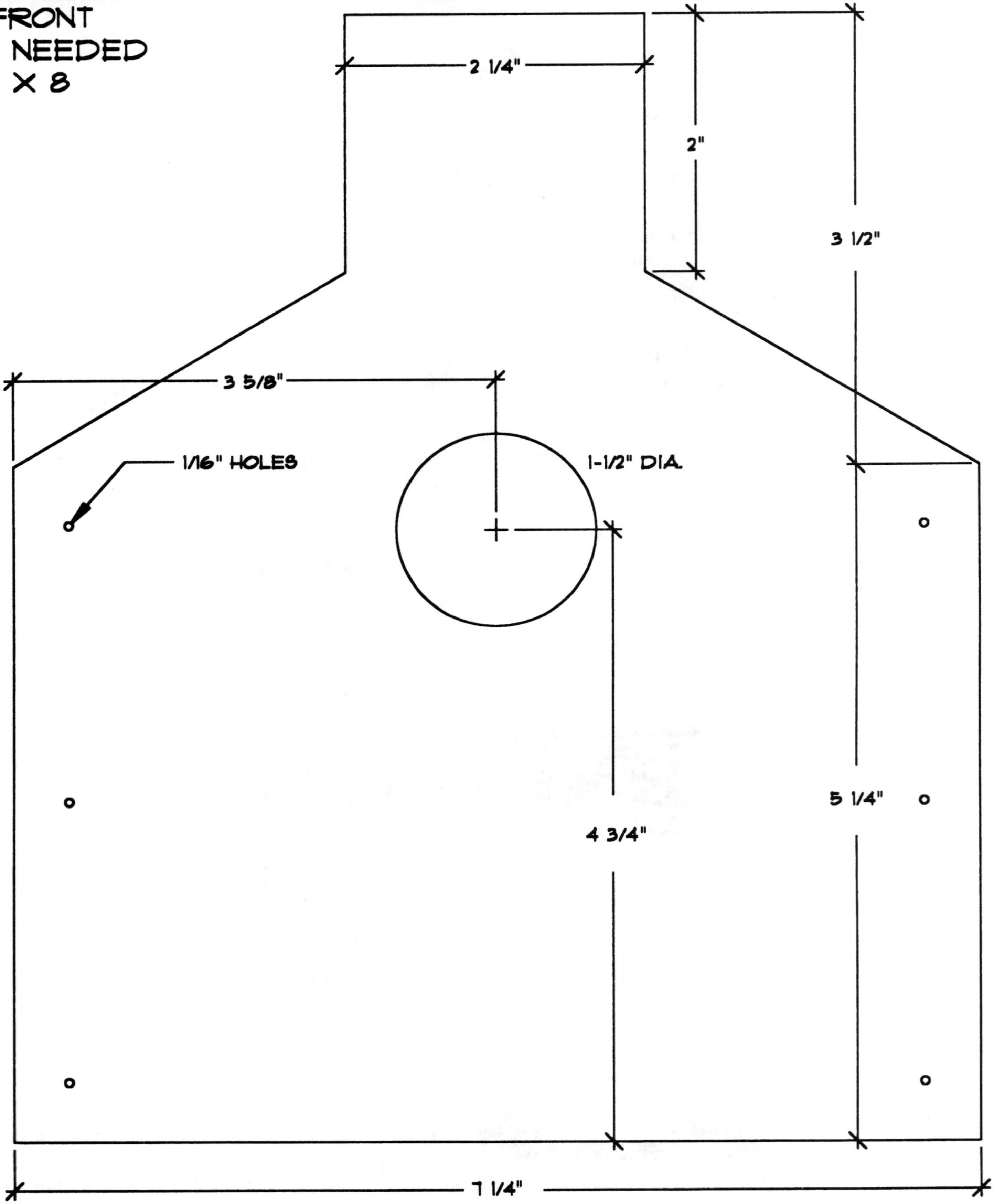

NEW ENGLAND CHURCH

BACK
1 NEEDED
1 X 8

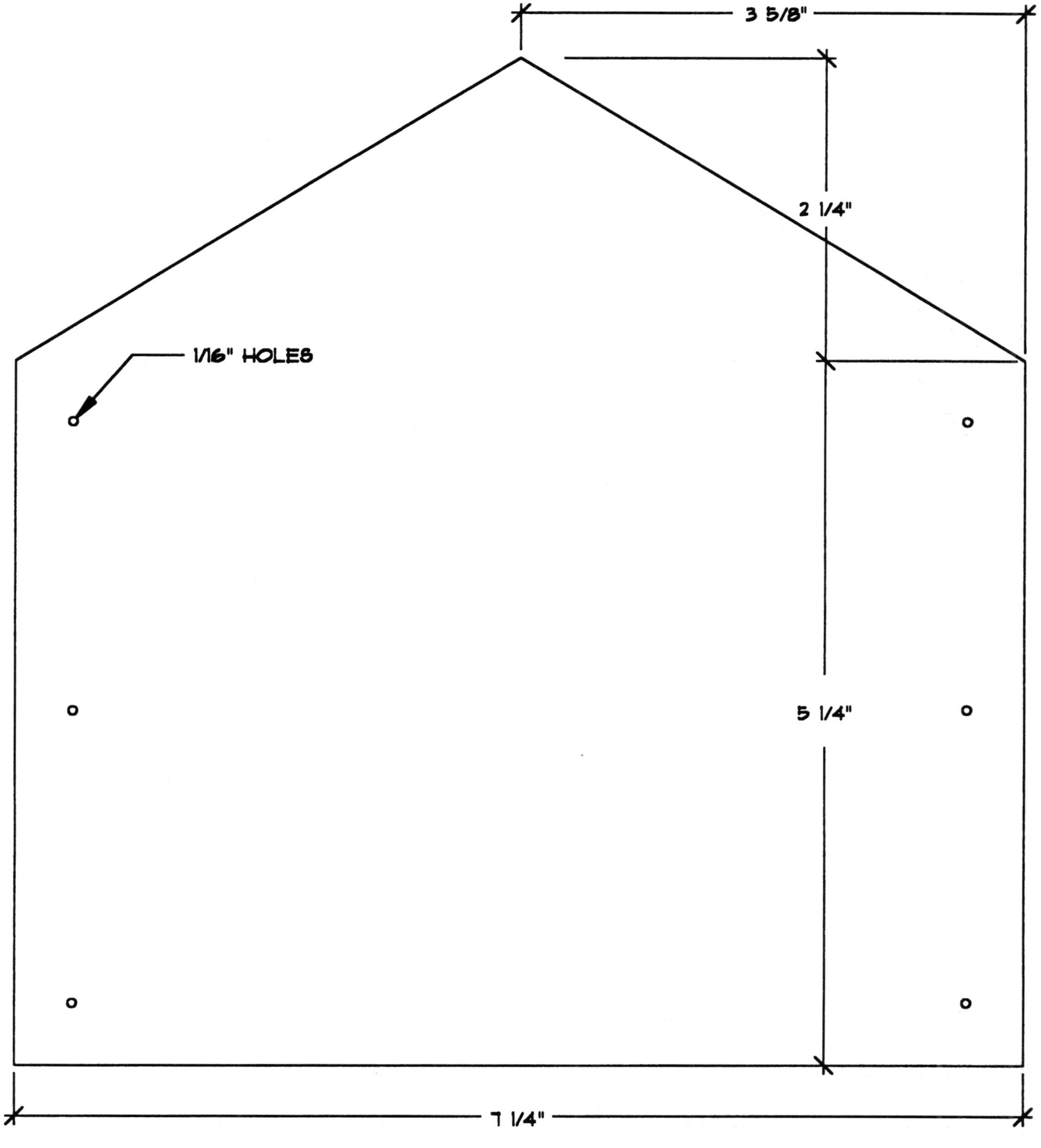

NEW ENGLAND CHURCH

INTERIOR PARTITION
1 NEEDED
1 X 8

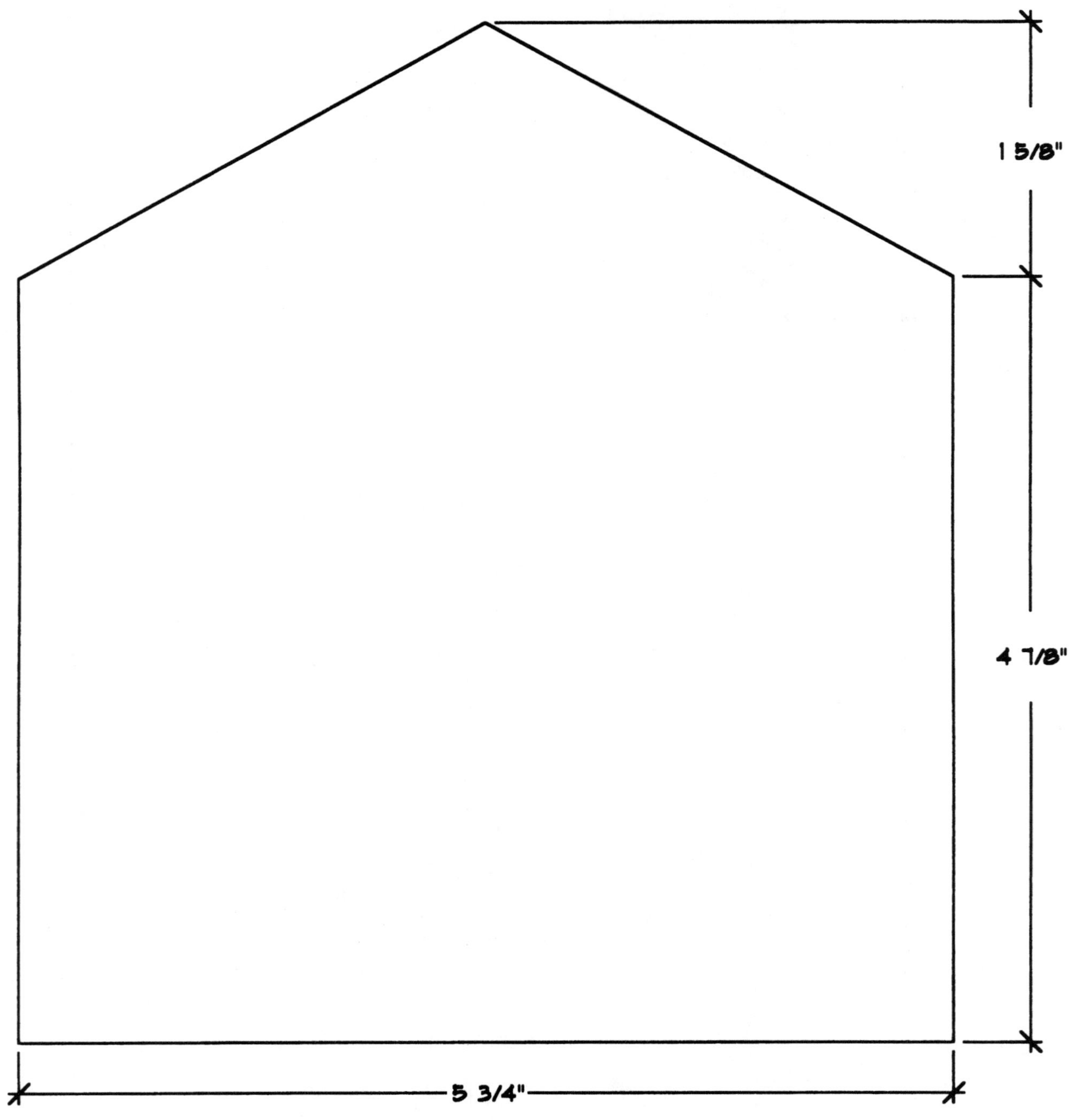

NEW ENGLAND CHURCH

SIDE WALL
2 NEEDED
1 X 8

NEW ENGLAND CHURCH

FLOOR
1 NEEDED
1 X 8

NEW ENGLAND CHURCH

STEEPLE PIECES
1 × 8

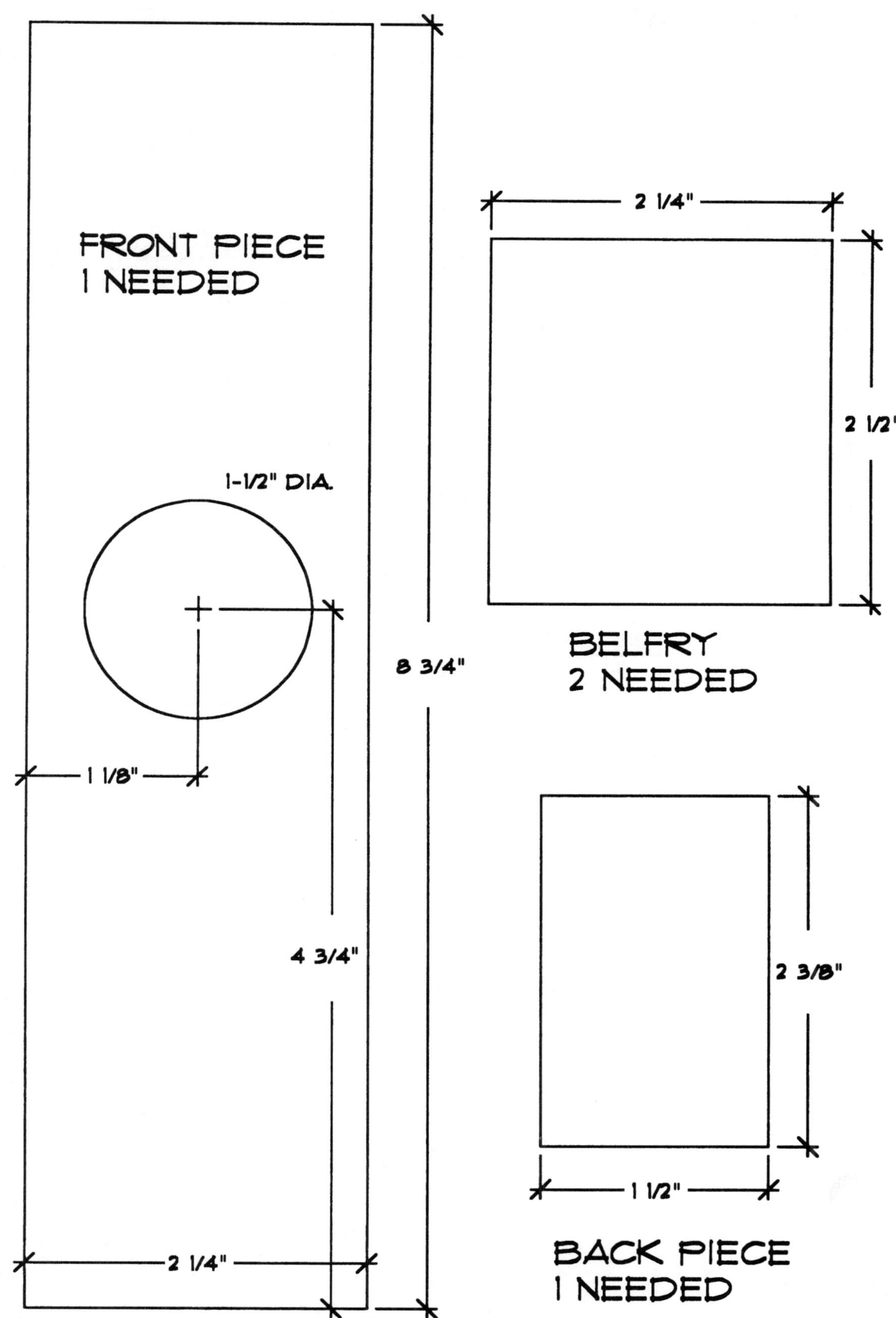

NEW ENGLAND CHURCH

STEEPLE PLATFORM
2 5/8" X 1/4" LATTICE

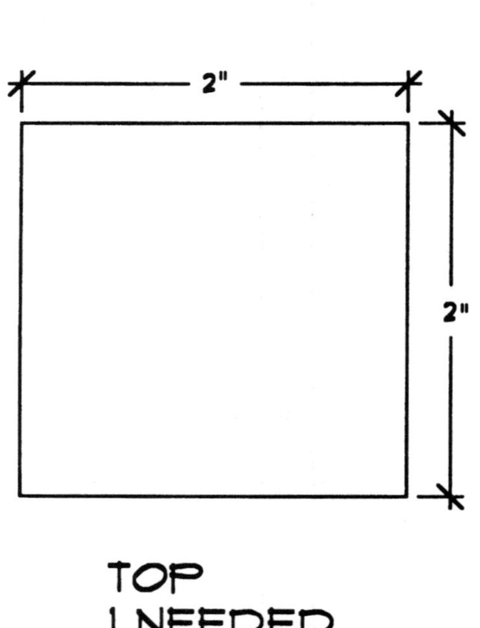

TOP
1 NEEDED

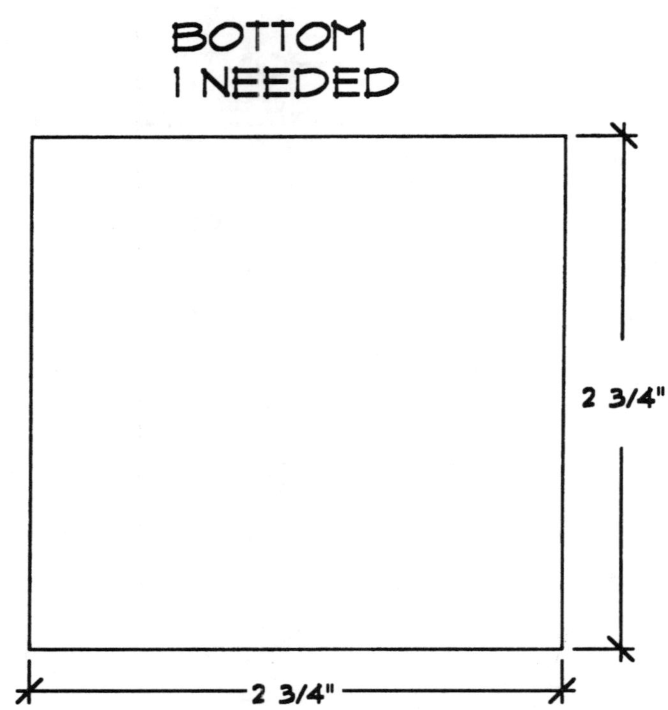

BOTTOM
1 NEEDED

NEW ENGLAND CHURCH

ROOF SECTIONS
2 NEEDED
1/4" PLYWOOD

1/2 scale

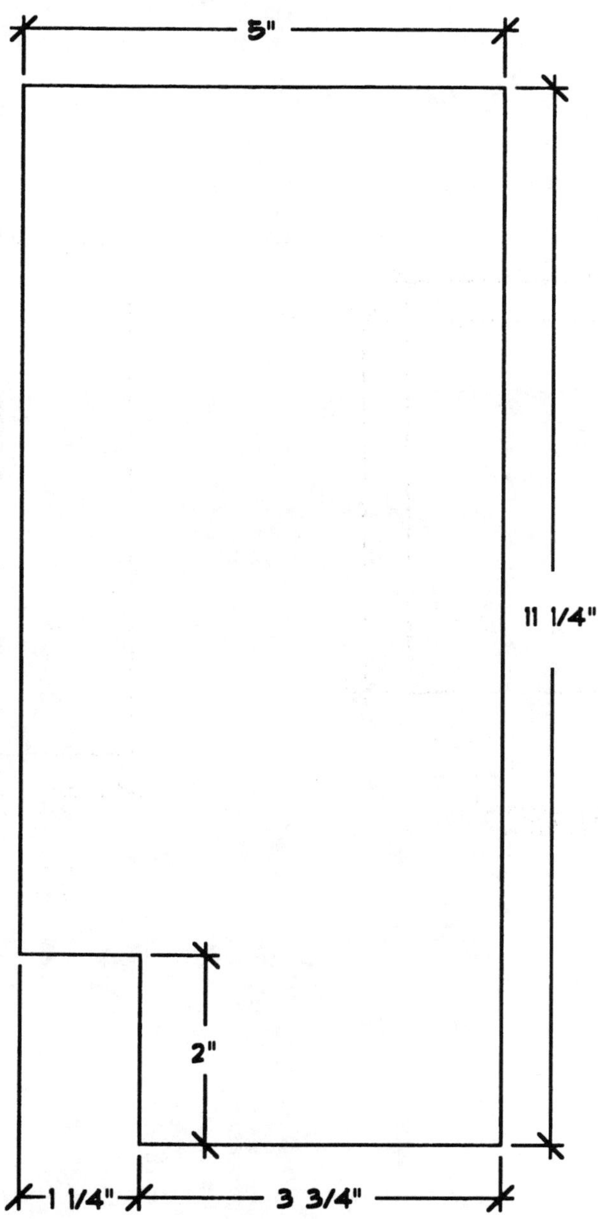

I grew up in this Cape Cod, about 500 miles away from the real Cape Cod. There wasn't much nautical about my home town, but the people there make the best hard pretzels in the known universe.

There are probably several billion variations on the basic Cape Cod design. If you have one that's near and dear to you, these plans should get the creative juices flowing.

This particular variation is designed for warblers, with a nesting area 5-3/4" square and 6" deep.

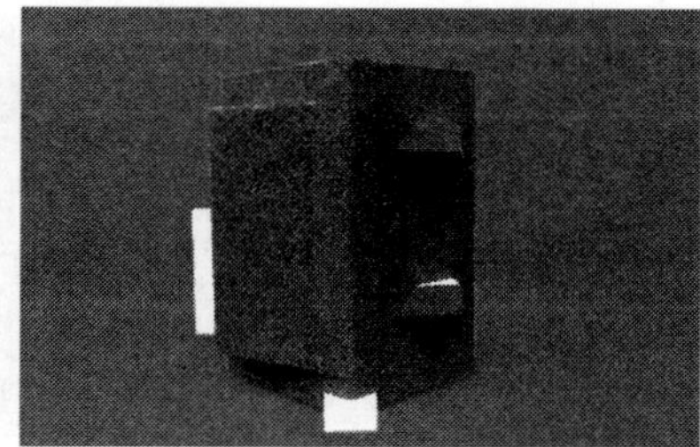
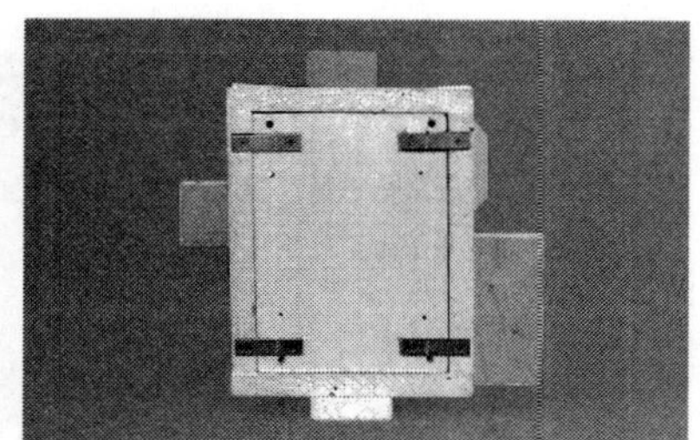

Materials list:

(2) 3-foot 1 x 8 boards

2-1/2 square feet of 1/4" or thinner plywood

Assorted 1/4" and 1/2" moldings (see photo for suggestions)

(1) fiberglass roofing shingle

4d galvanized finish nails

4d galvanized common nails (to attach roof)

3/4" 16 ga. brads (preferably galvanized)

7/16" aluminum or copper tacks (to attach roof shingle)

Type II weatherproof glue

(4) brass mending plates with brass screws

Latex waterproof caulk

Exterior primer and paint

Special tool required: Miter box

Instructions:

For instructions on how this birdhouse is built, refer to the Building Basics section.

What is not covered in Building Basics is the assembly of the back and front dormer windows:

Begin by cutting all pieces except the back dormer ends. Cut entrance hole and assemble four walls per instructions in Building Basics section.

Front dormers:

1. Cut front dormer pieces from waste from end parts — the angles are perfect.

2. Glue front dormer pieces together — two per dormer. When glue has dried, sand the dormers to assure uniformity and a flat surface on the face. Place each dormer in a miter box and cut two 45-degree angles to form the roof peak on each dormer.

3. Place the front dormers 1-1/8" up from bottom of front roof, 2" in from ends of front roof. Tape in place using strong tape such as duct tape.

4. Drill 1/16" holes from inside of roof into back of front dormers. Make sure the holes are deep enough to accommodate the length of brads.

5. Remove tape and front dormers. Place brads through holes in roof from the inside out.

6. Spread glue on back of front dormers. Press into place and hold tightly for a few minutes until glue grabs.

Back dormer:

1. Cut paper template for back dormer ends and check to see that the angles work. (If your end-part cutting is off just little, the back dormer end will not work as drawn in these plans without some minor modification.)

2. When you are satisfied that the back dormer ends will work, cut them from wood.

3. Attach back dormer ends to back wall using nails or screws and glue. Before you attach them, make sure the angle will put the peak at the right place in relation to the end-wall roof peak. Glue the dormer ends to the end walls. When glue is dry, fill any gaps on the roof side with caulk. Fill any gaps on the wall side with spackle.

When all of the above steps are completed, the roof pieces may be attached.

Left: side door.

Below: back door.

CAPE COD

ENDS - 2 NEEDED (ACCESS HOLE IN 1)
DORMERS
1 X 8

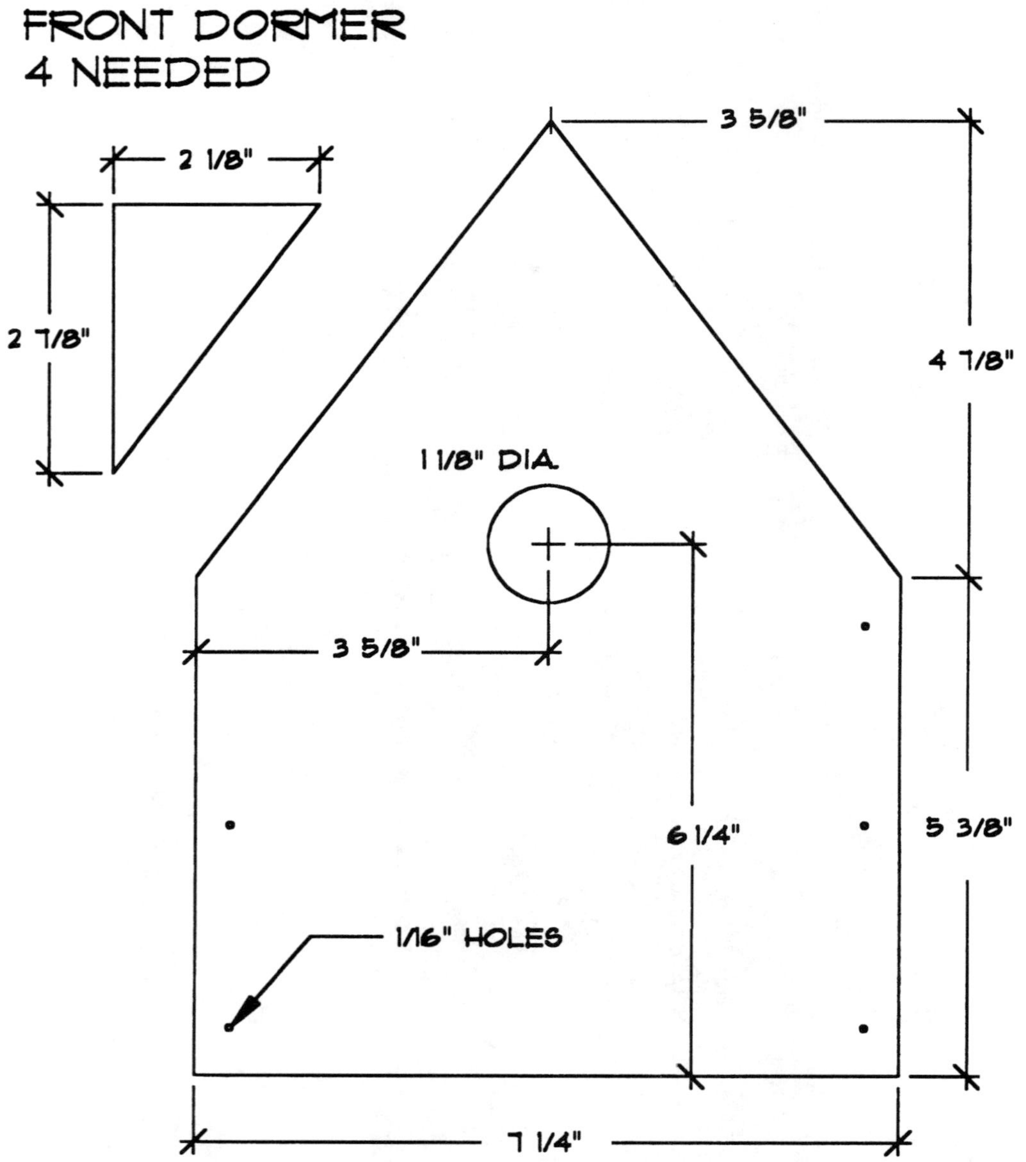

FRONT DORMER
4 NEEDED

2 1/8"

2 7/8"

3 5/8"

4 7/8"

1 1/8" DIA.

3 5/8"

6 1/4"

5 3/8"

1/16" HOLES

7 1/4"

CAPE COD
INTERIOR PARTITION
DORMERS

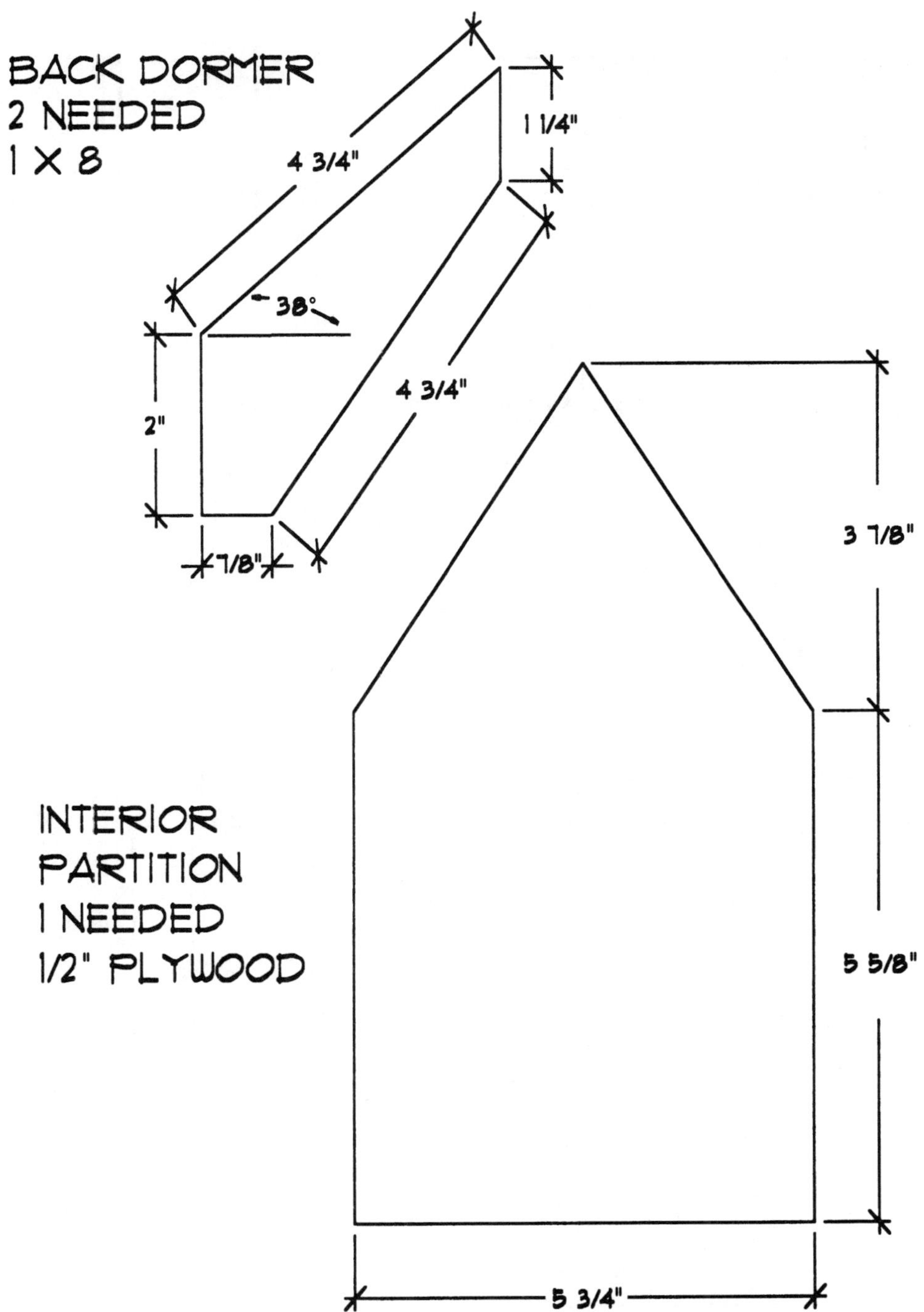

CAPE COD
WALLS - 1 X 8

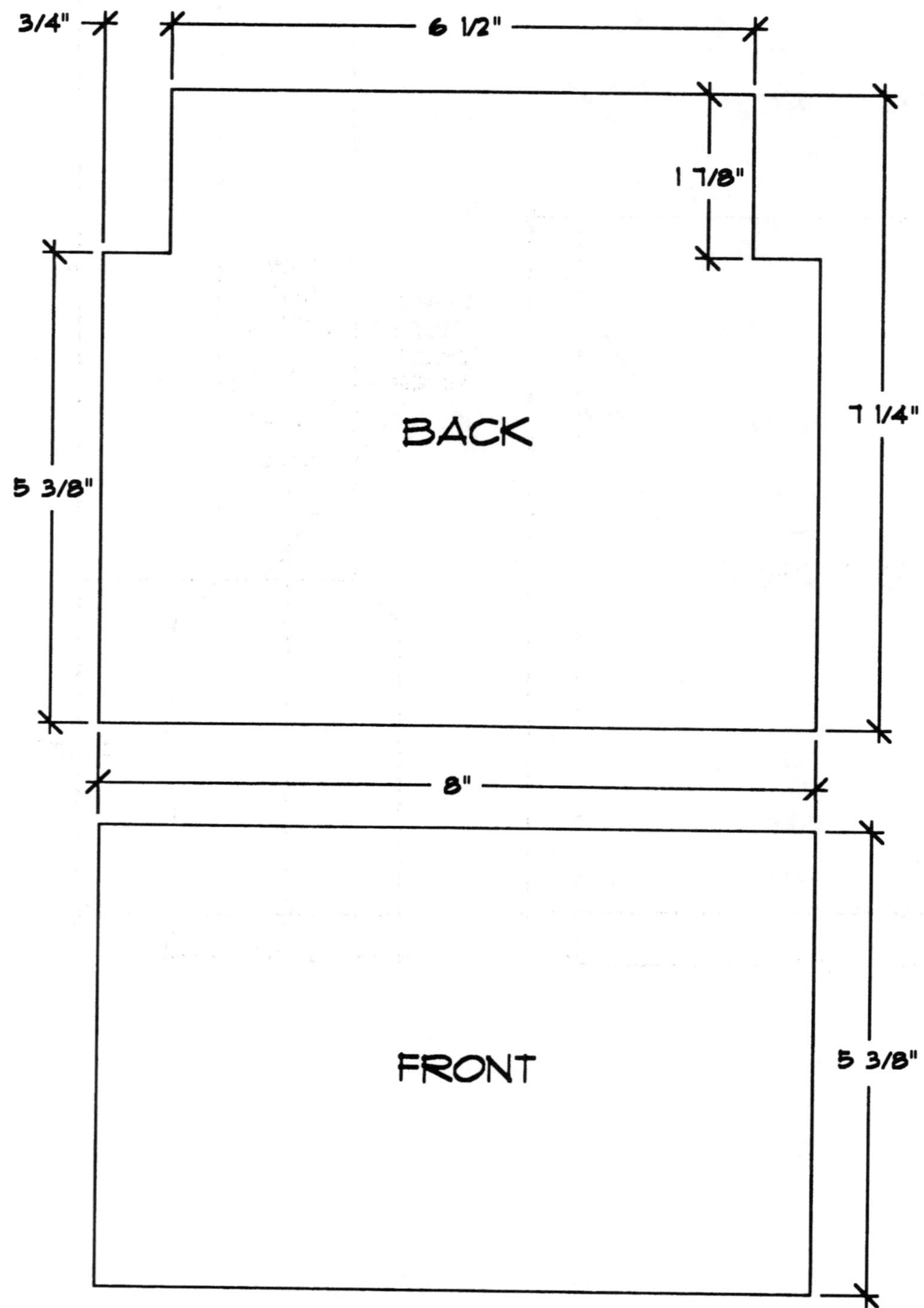

CAPE COD

CHIMNEY & FLOOR
1 X 8

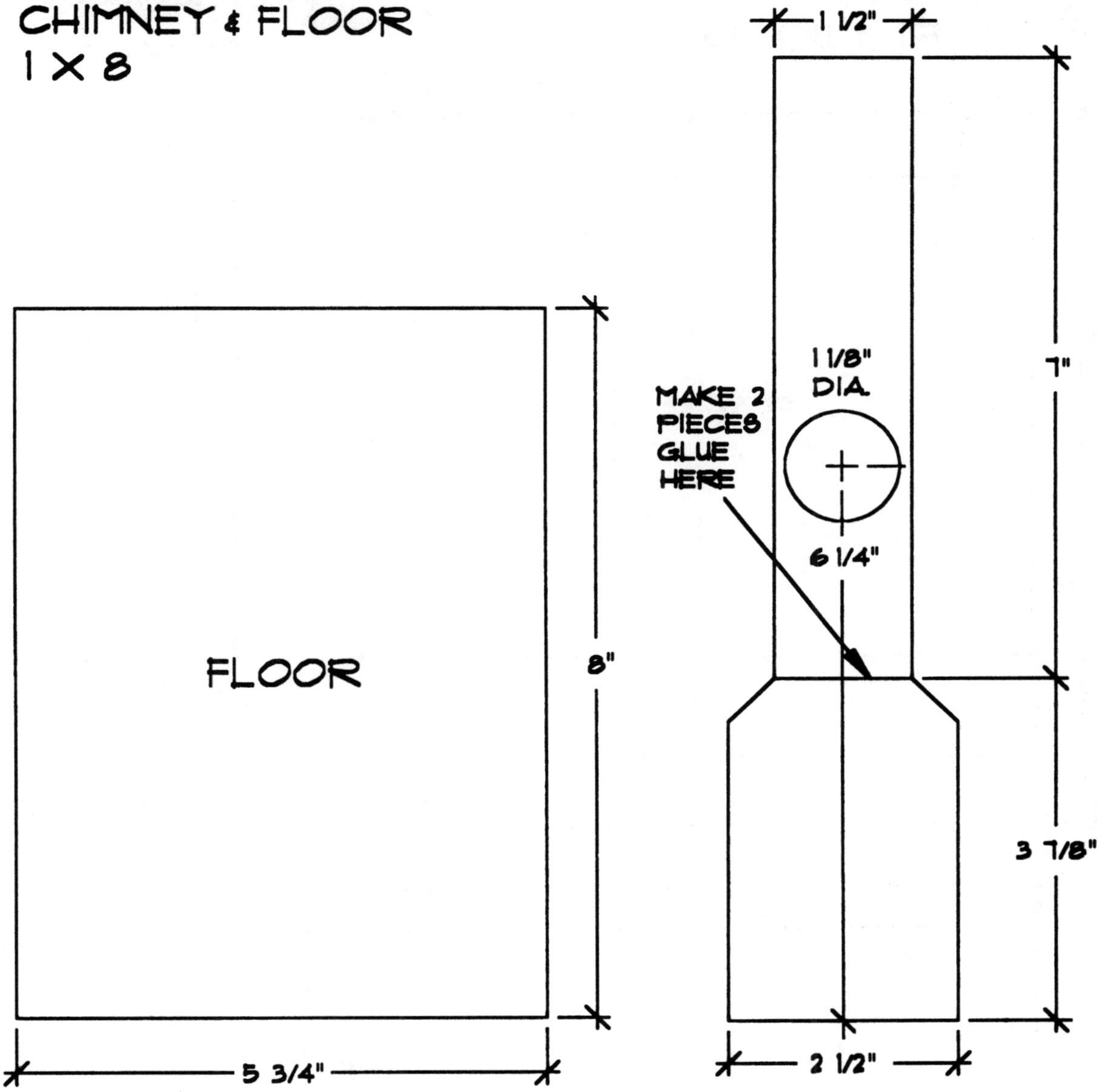

CAPE COD
ROOF - 1/4" PLYWOOD

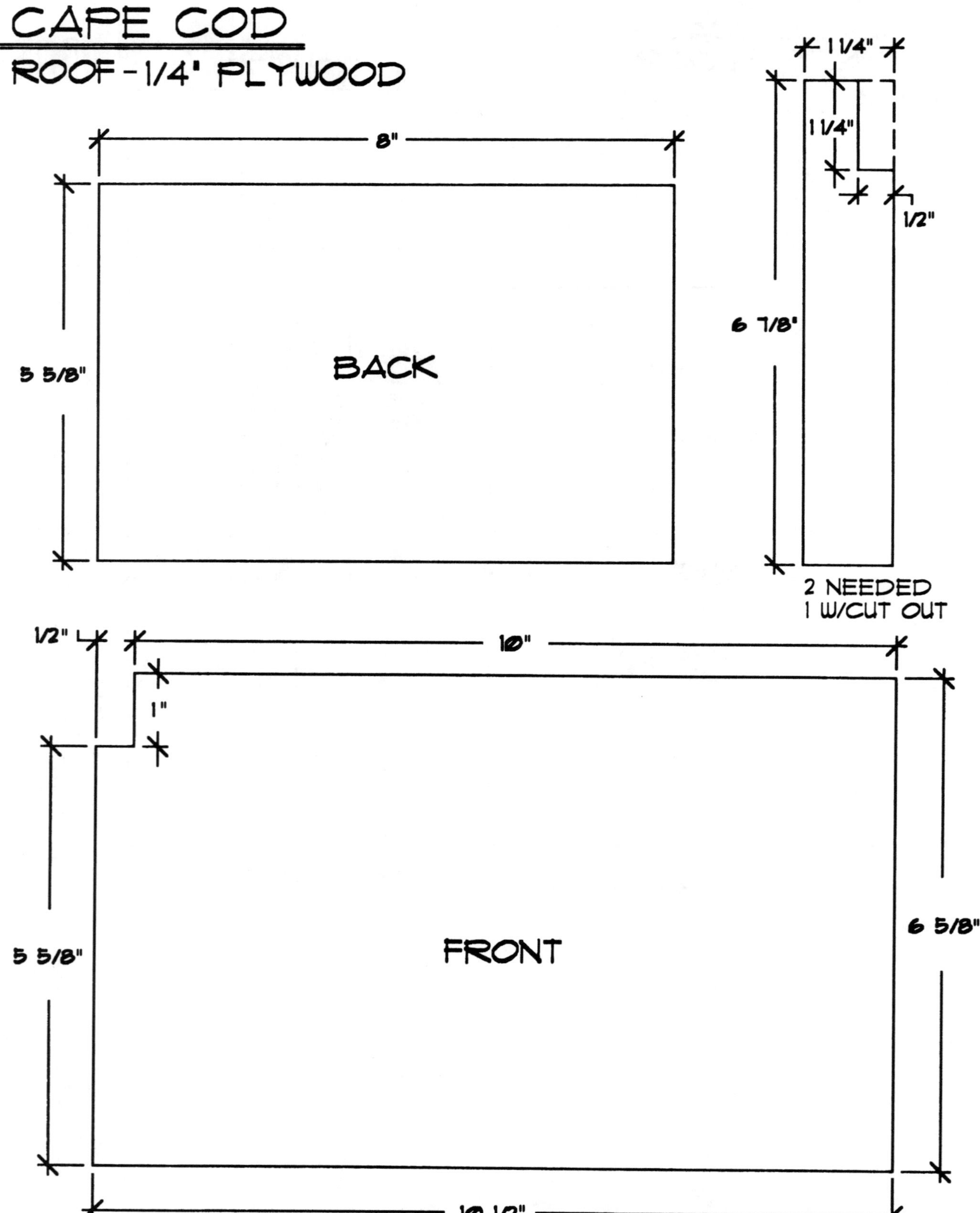

CAPE COD

PORCHES
1 X 8

FRONT PORCH
FRONT VIEW

FRONT PORCH
SIDE VIEW

SIDE PORCH
FRONT VIEW

SIDE PORCH
SIDE VIEW

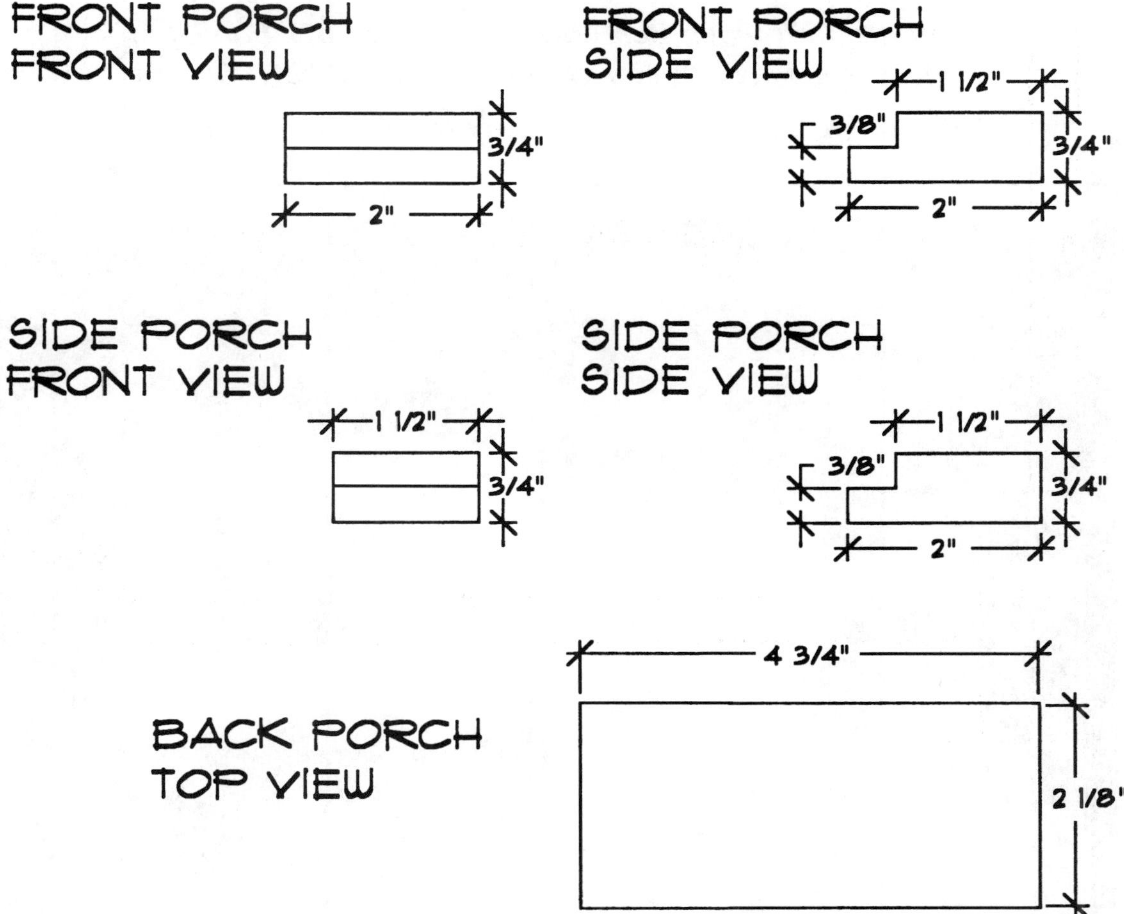

BACK PORCH
TOP VIEW

ROXBOROUGH ROW HOUSE

If you know people who live in Philadelphia, they probably see more row houses in a month than most people see in a lifetime.

The styles of Philly row houses range from the elegant Society Hill colonials built when Ben Franklin lived in the 'hood, to the modernesque style-free brick boxes built in the 1950s and 60s.

This design is a modest 1930s variation on a familiar theme.

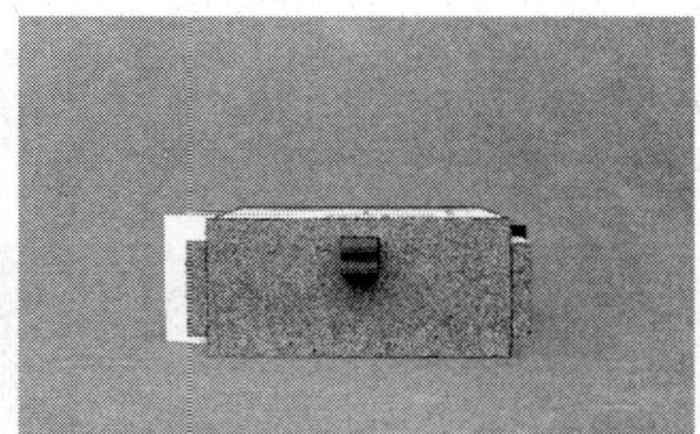
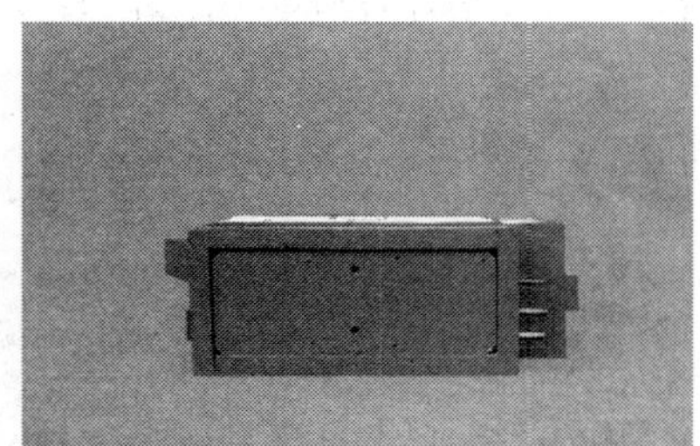

Materials list:

(1) 3-foot 1 x 12 board

(1) 6-foot 1 x 6 board

1 foot of 1/4" lattice

(12) # 8 x 1-1/2" brass wood screws

(26) # 6 x 1-1/4" brass wood screws   (more if you plan to use screws to attach the porch, etc.)

Type II weatherproof glue

Latex waterproof caulk

Exterior primer and paint

Dollhouse wallpaper and paneling (optional)

Instructions:

For basic instructions on how this birdhouse is built, refer to the Building Basics section.

What is not covered in Building Basics is the order in which the pieces of this structure go together.

1. Cut out all parts, including porches, dormers, etc. Drill all holes.

2. Cut entrance holes.

3. Attach front and rear dormers.

4. Cut recessed doors and windows, if any.

5. Attach the front porch roof using screws and glue. You will attach the porch after you have put the final coat of paint on the front of the house.

6. Assemble the four walls of the house using screws and glue.

7. Glue chimney parts together. When glue is dry, drill vent holes.

8. Attach inner partitions.

9. Attach roof and chimney.

10. Attach floor.

11. Paint the front, back and sides. Use wall paper and paneling on the sides.

12. Attach porches and cellar steps.

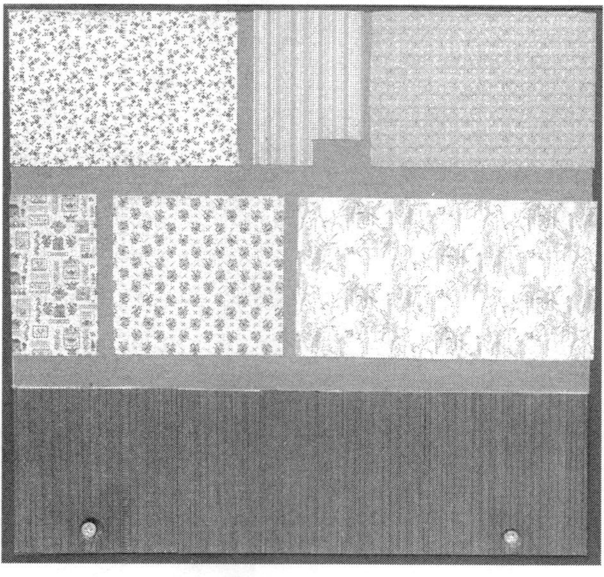

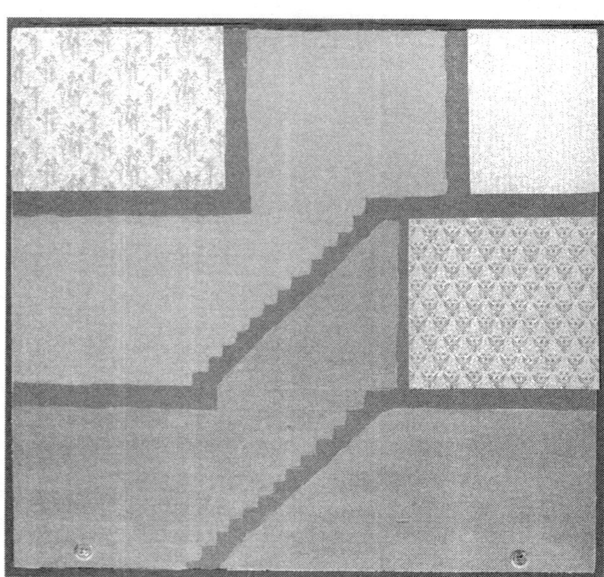

ROXBOROUGH ROW HOUSE

STRUCTURAL PARTS
1 X 6

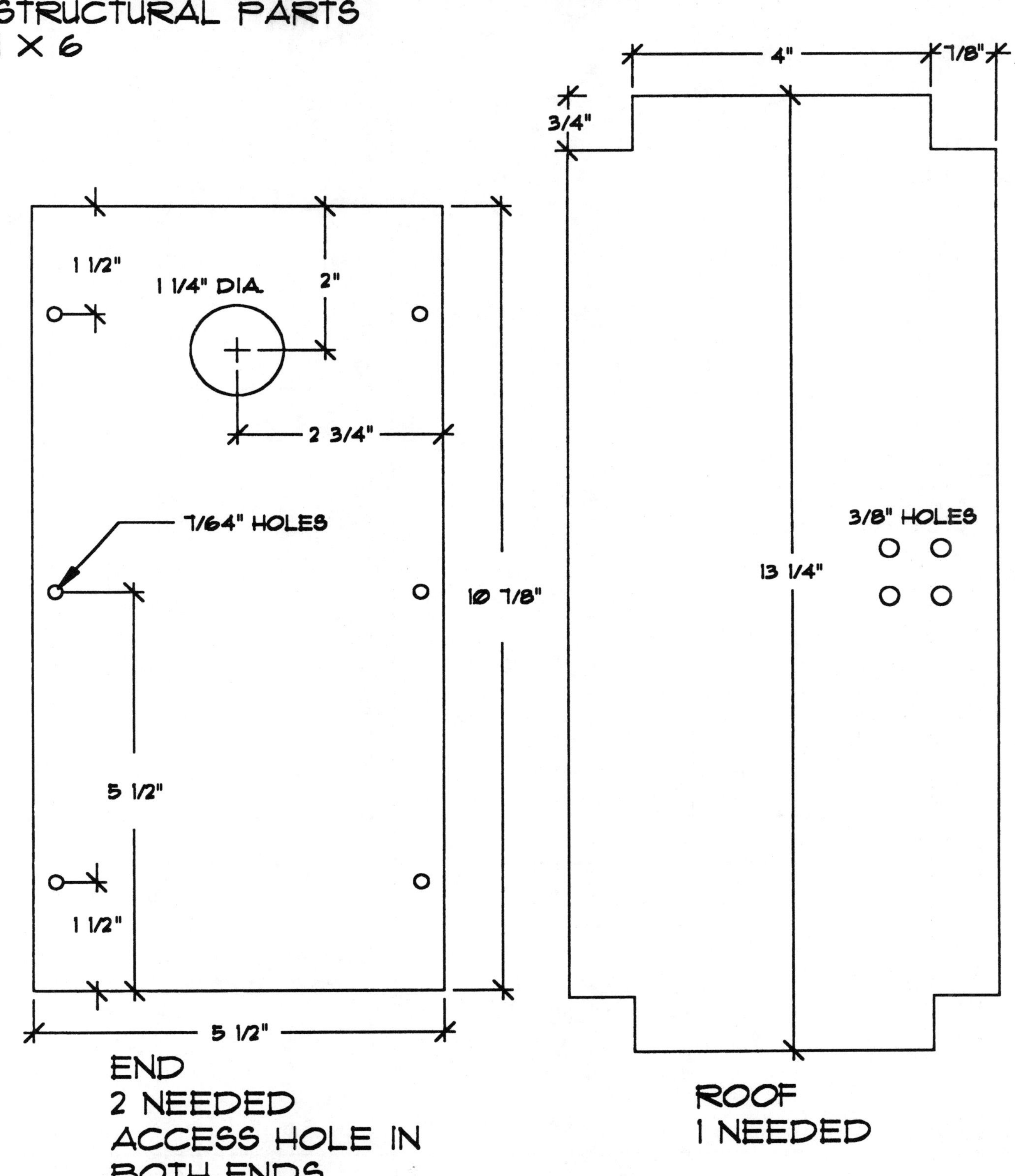

ROXBOROUGH ROW HOUSE

STRUCTURAL PARTS
1 X 12

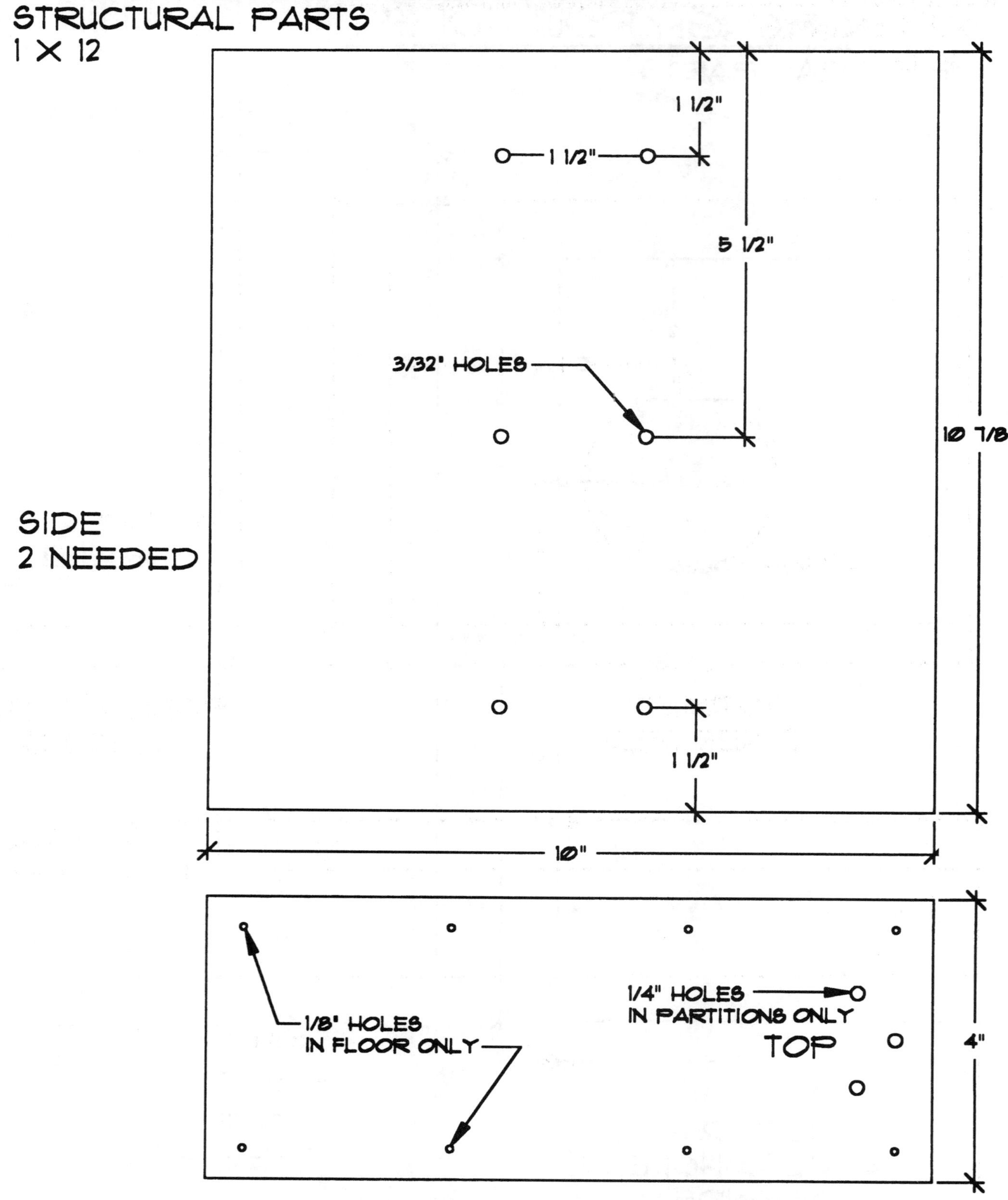

FLOOR & PARTITIONS (1 X 6)
3 NEEDED
(1 FLOOR, 2 PARTITIONS)

ROXBOROUGH ROW HOUSE

TRIM PARTS
1 X 6

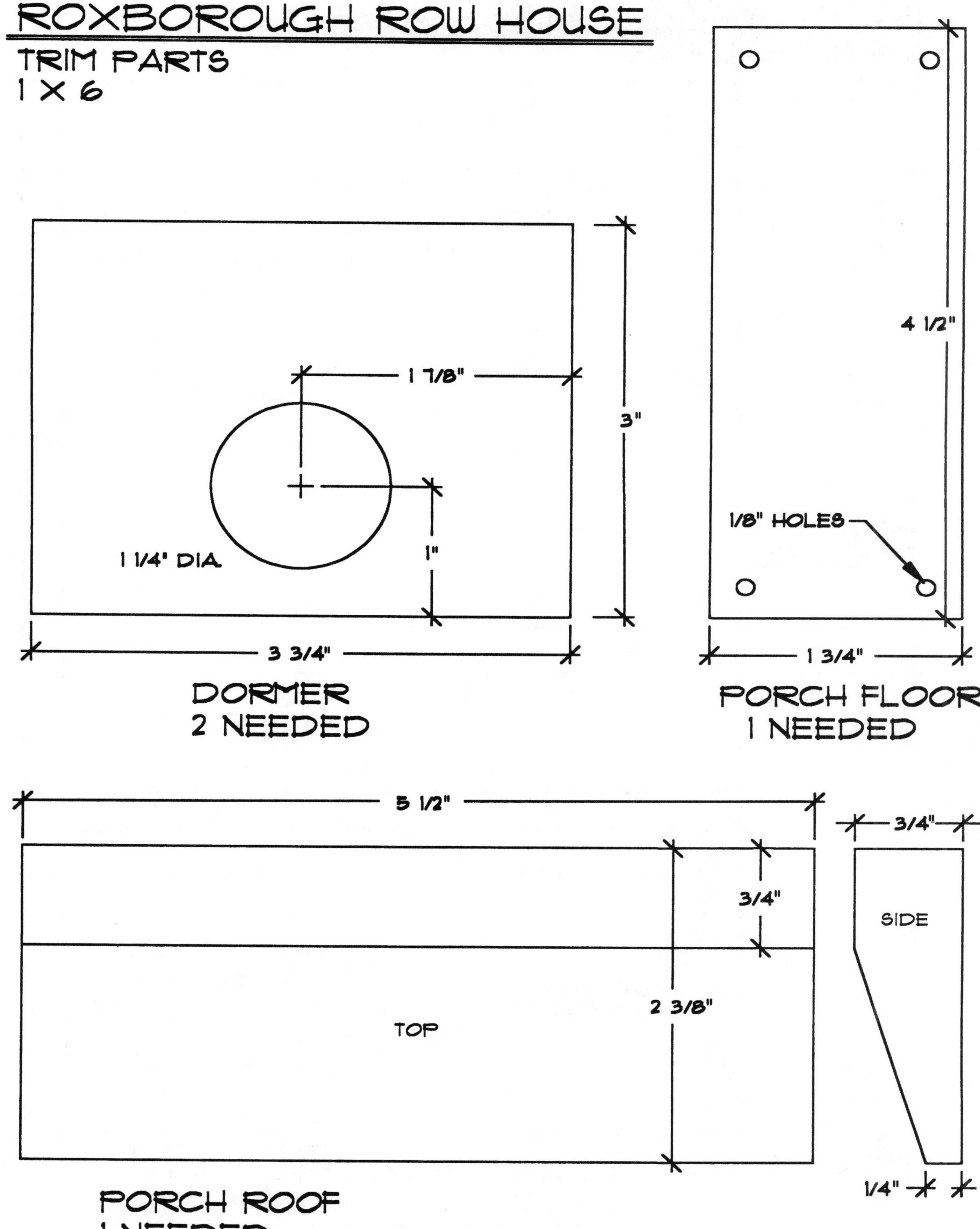

ROXBOROUGH ROW HOUSE

TRIM PARTS
1 X 6, LATTICE

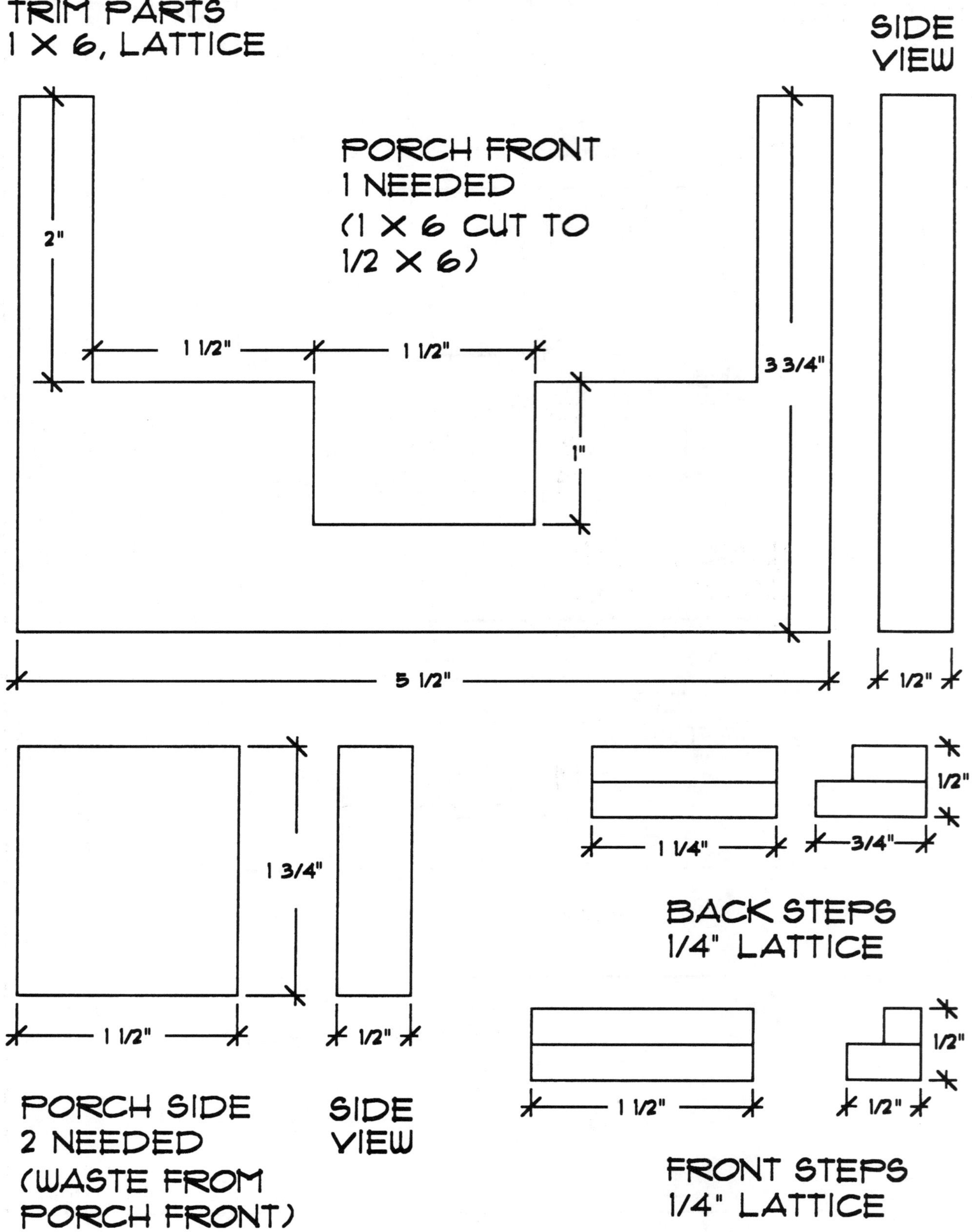

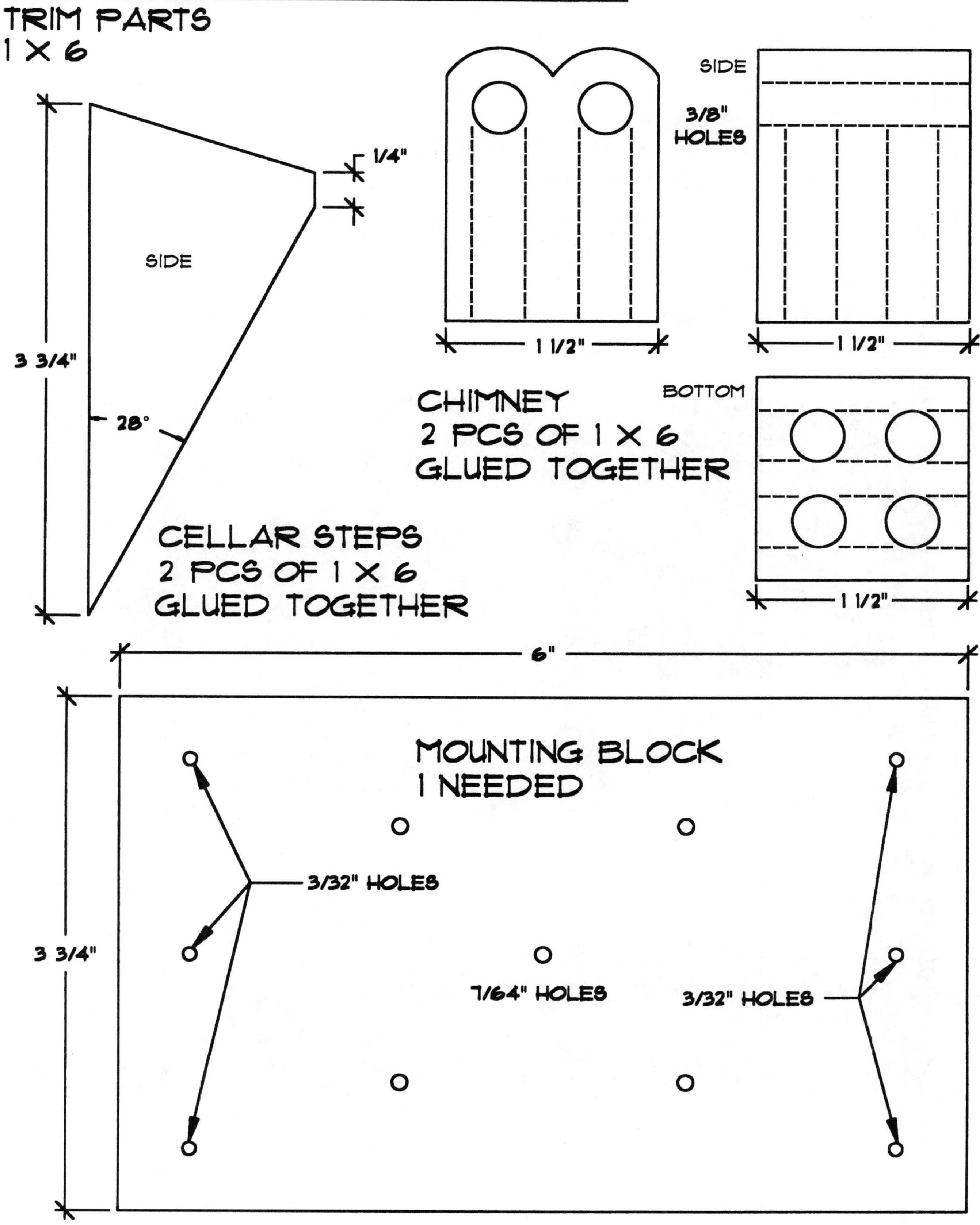

ROXBOROUGH ROW HOUSE
TRIM PARTS
1 X 6
SIDE
1/4"
3 3/4"
28°
SIDE
3/8" HOLES
1 1/2"
CHIMNEY
2 PCS OF 1 X 6
GLUED TOGETHER
BOTTOM
1 1/2"
CELLAR STEPS
2 PCS OF 1 X 6
GLUED TOGETHER
6"
MOUNTING BLOCK
1 NEEDED
3/32" HOLES
7/64" HOLES
3/32" HOLES
3 3/4"

CRACKERBOX PALACE

Hats off to the person who invented the house on wheels. This amazing device has allowed millions of us to put home where the heart is with a minimum of hassle. It has also allowed millions more of us to have a home we might otherwise go without.

During my 19th year in this world, I lived in two of these mobile homes, one in Pennsylvania and one in Mississippi. Both were filled with love and fun.

This one is designed to accommodate four families of Purple Martins.

Materials list:

(2) 6-foot 1 x 8 boards

6 feet of 2-5/8" x 1/4" lattice

43" of 3/4" quarter-round molding

Assorted moldings (see photo for suggestions)

4d galvanized finish nails

3/4" 16 ga. brads (preferably galvanized)

(20) #8 1-1/2" brass wood screws

(2) 3/4" brass or brass plated angle irons and screws

Type II weatherproof glue

Exterior primer and paint

Instructions:

To build this birdhouse, use the following steps.

Note: I strongly recommend using screws instead of nails to assemble the structural parts.

1. Cut out all structural parts.

2. Cut entrance holes in sides. You can put them all on one side but I think it looks better with only two per side.

Drill a single 1/4" hole 1/4" from the top edge of the wall opposite each entrance hole. You will need to cut a channel in the roof trim to vent the 1/4" hole you just drilled. (see photo above)

3. Assemble the four walls. The side walls go inside the end walls. Use the screw method covered in item 7 of the Building Basics section. I recommend three screws per joint. Remember to drill countersinks before you drill the holes.

4. While the glue on your four walls is setting, start making the roof. First you want to glue the roof peak to the roof leaving 3/4" at the front end for the quarter round molding.

5. When the glue holding the roof peak is set, glue the quarter round molding in place. The molding is placed at the front and back of the roof peak and under each end of the roof flush with the outer edge of the roof.

6. When the glue holding the quarter round pieces is set, attach the side piece lattice. Start by lining up the top of the

lattice with the top and front of the roof (remember, the front is where the towing hitch would go). Drill 1/16" holes and tack the lattice in place with brads. On the inside face of the lattice, mark where the lattice needs to be cut to conform to the roof outline. Carefully cut the lattice to the proper shape. (Lattice is very easy to cut and shape. You may want to cut your quarter round shapes using a file and sandpaper while the lattice is in place.) Repeat for the other side. Glue and nail the lattice in place using 4d galvanized finish nails.

7. Fit the roof over the house and note where the 1/4" ventilation holes are. Remove the roof. Using a chisel, cut channels to allow the ventilation holes to vent to the outside once the roof is installed permanently.

8. Attach the inner partitions. Start by drilling 1/16" holes from the outside wall in to the partition. Use two per side of each partition. Nail each partition in place with 4d finish nails. Glue is not necessary.

9. Attach the floor. With the structure upside down, put the floor in place and drill countersink and screw holes. Use screws without glue to attach the floor. This floor will be removable for cleaning.

10. Fill all holes and cracks with exterior grade spackle. Sand smooth.

11. Remove the floor and prime the structure and roof with exterior grade primer keeping the primer THIN where the roof will fit down over the structure.

12. Finish paint all parts of the structure.

13. Attach the roof permanently using one angle iron at each end, inside the bird house.

14. Attach the floor.

15. Attach any decoration or molding. The trim around the outside of the one I built is shelf-edge molding. The windows are lattice cut with a chisel to resemble jalousie windows, set in to recessed windows made with a chisel. The doors are outlined with thin strips of wood and the door knobs are round pieces of wood. The TV antenna is brass rod, soldered together and painted silver. The chimney is wood painted silver.

CRACKERBOX PALACE

STRUCTURAL PARTS
1 X 8

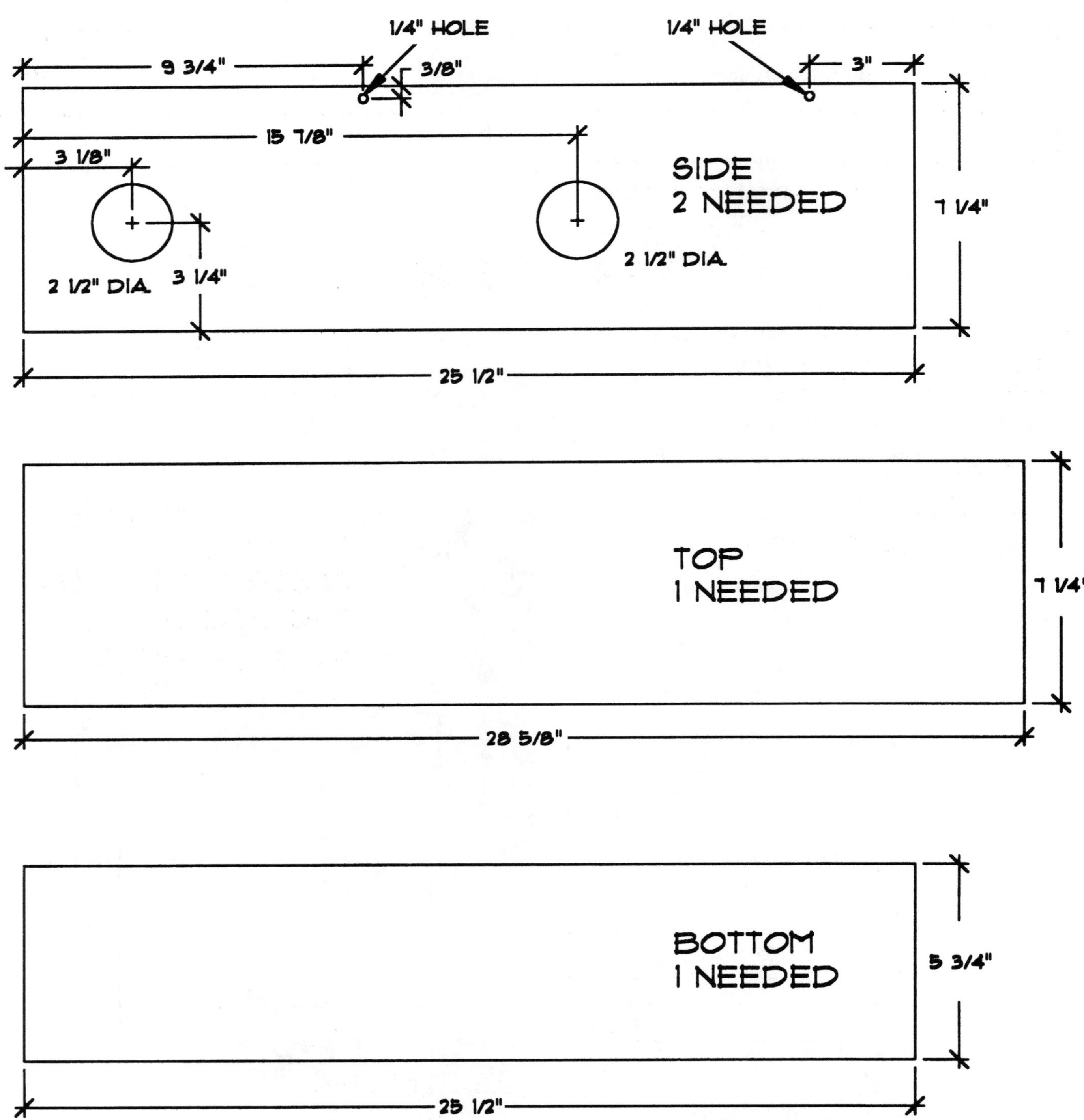

CRACKERBOX PALACE
STRUCTURAL & TRIM PARTS

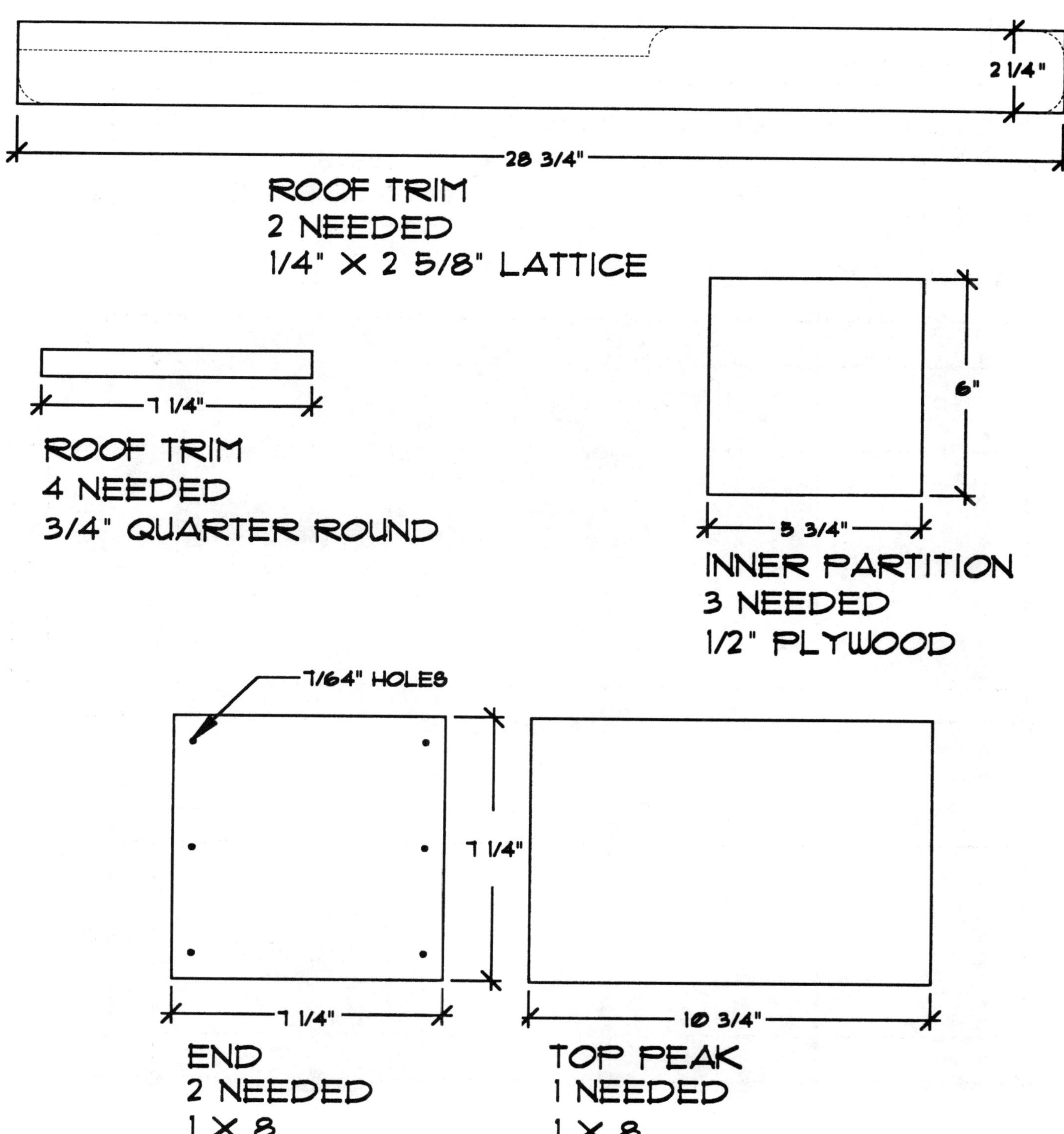

Cruise around the Green Mountains of Vermont long enough and you're sure to see one of these. In fact you're likely to see one of these just about anywhere out in the country. It's a popular design because it's functional and cozy. I visited this one a while back. I don't have a snapshot so these plans were created using the Mind's Eye method.

The people who live there are very careful about recycling. In their honor, this chickadee house is made entirely of recycled grape crates. It has three nesting areas, each about 4" square and 8" deep.

  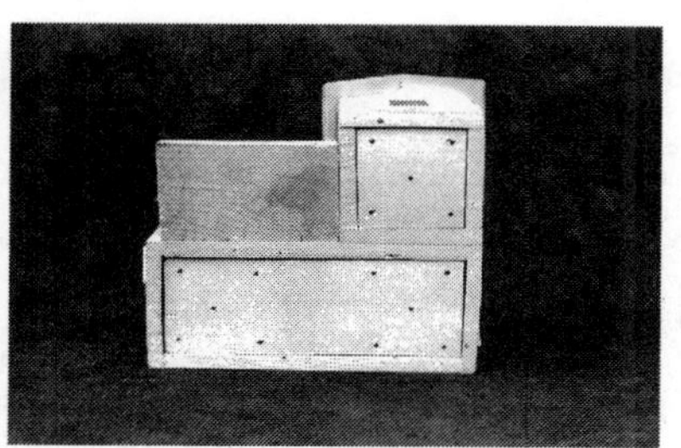

Materials list:

(5) grape crates like the ones pictured in the "Found Wood" section. You're going to need 97-3/8" of wood; you get 23-3/4" from each crate and you need to allow for waste such as knots and cupping. The grape crates will also supply the 1/8" underlayment for the roof.

(2) Roofing shingles

4-1/2" of 3/8" quarter-round molding

4d galvanized common nails

4d galvanized finish nails

(4) # 6 1" brass wood screws

7/16" aluminum or copper tacks (to attach roof shingles)

Latex waterproof caulk

Type II weatherproof wood glue

Exterior primer and paint

Instructions:

For instructions on how this birdhouse is built, refer to the *Building Basics* section.

What is not covered in *Building Basics* is how this structure, which is essentially two birdhouses, goes together.

1. After you have cut all structural pieces and cut the entrance holes, build the small birdhouse first. Position the pieces so that the "bellies" if the wood is cupped are facing to the outside. Place the side walls inside the end walls and attach the walls using the techniques in the *Building Basics* section.

2. Attach the inner partitions to the inside side wall of the long birdhouse (the inside wall is the one facing the small birdhouse section. Two nails for each, without glue, is adequate.

3. Attach the inside side wall of the long birdhouse to the small birdhouse. Leave a 5/8" recess for the end of the long birdhouse. Use brass screws and glue.

4. Attach both ends of the long birdhouse.

5. Attach the long outside wall.

6. Attach the inner partitions to the outside wall.

7. Glue 1-1/2" pieces of 3/8" quarter round 1" below the center of the entrance hole.

8. Follow steps 9 through 24 in the *Building Basics* section.

9. The flower boxes are made of wood with bent, painted nails as flowers.

GREEN MOUNTAIN RANCH

ENDS - 4 NEEDED
(ACCESS HOLE IN 3)
5/8" LUMBER (FROM
   CRATE)

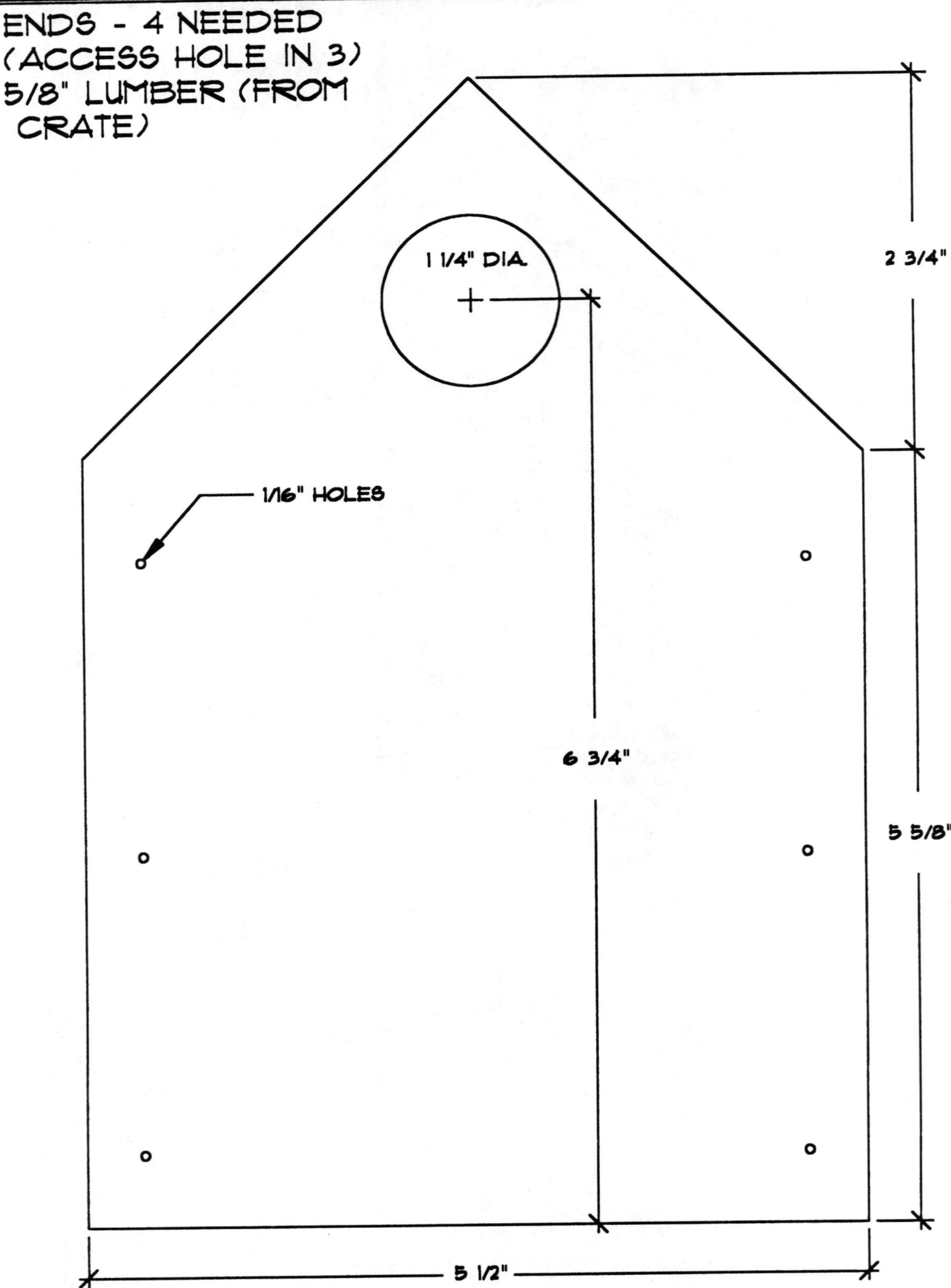

GREEN MOUNTAIN RANCH

INTERIOR PARTITION
2 NEEDED
5/8" LUMBER (FROM CRATE)

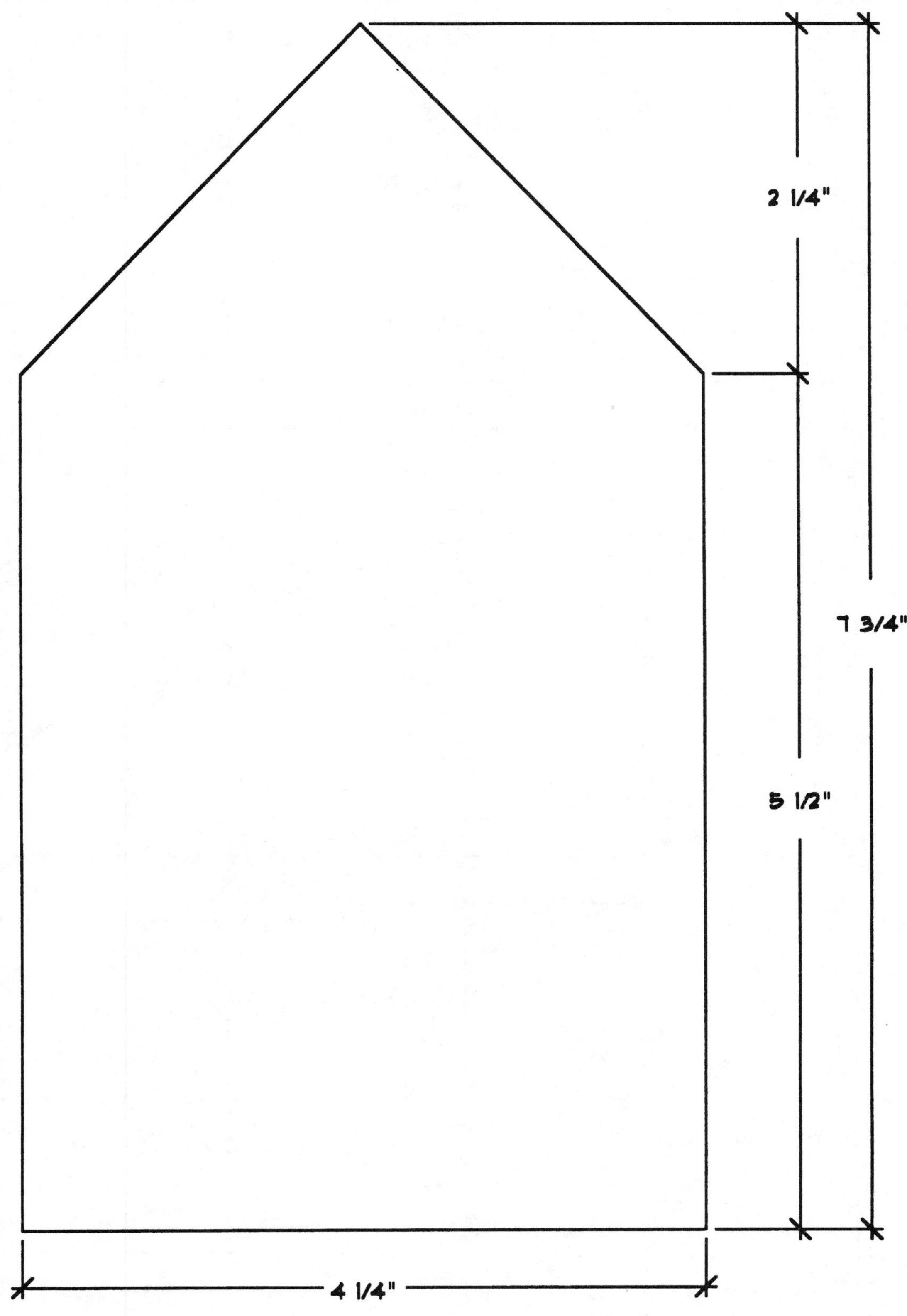

FLOORS & WALLS
5/8" LUMBER (FROM CRATE)

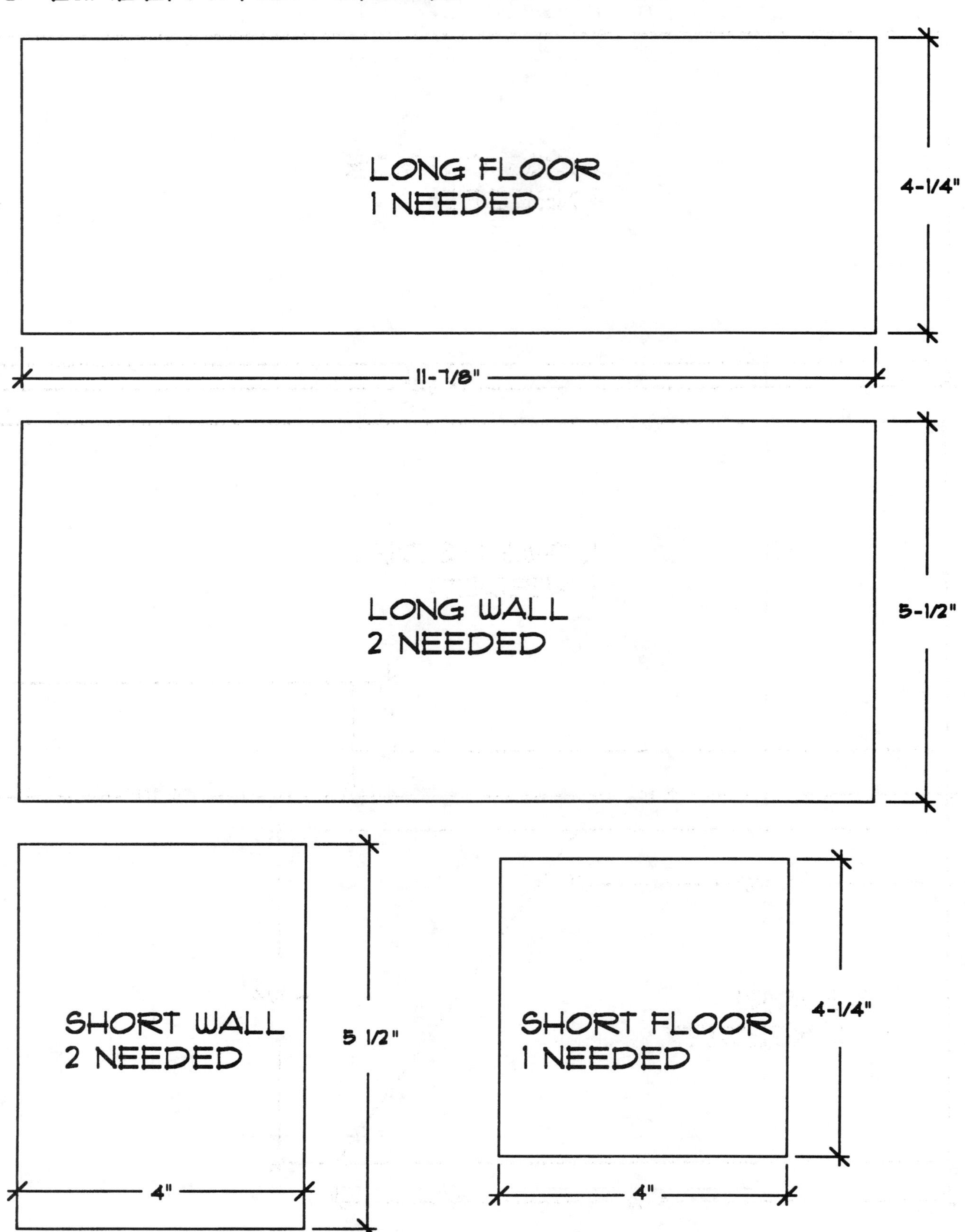

GREEN MOUNTAIN RANCH

ROOF PIECES
1/8" LUMBER (FROM CRATE)

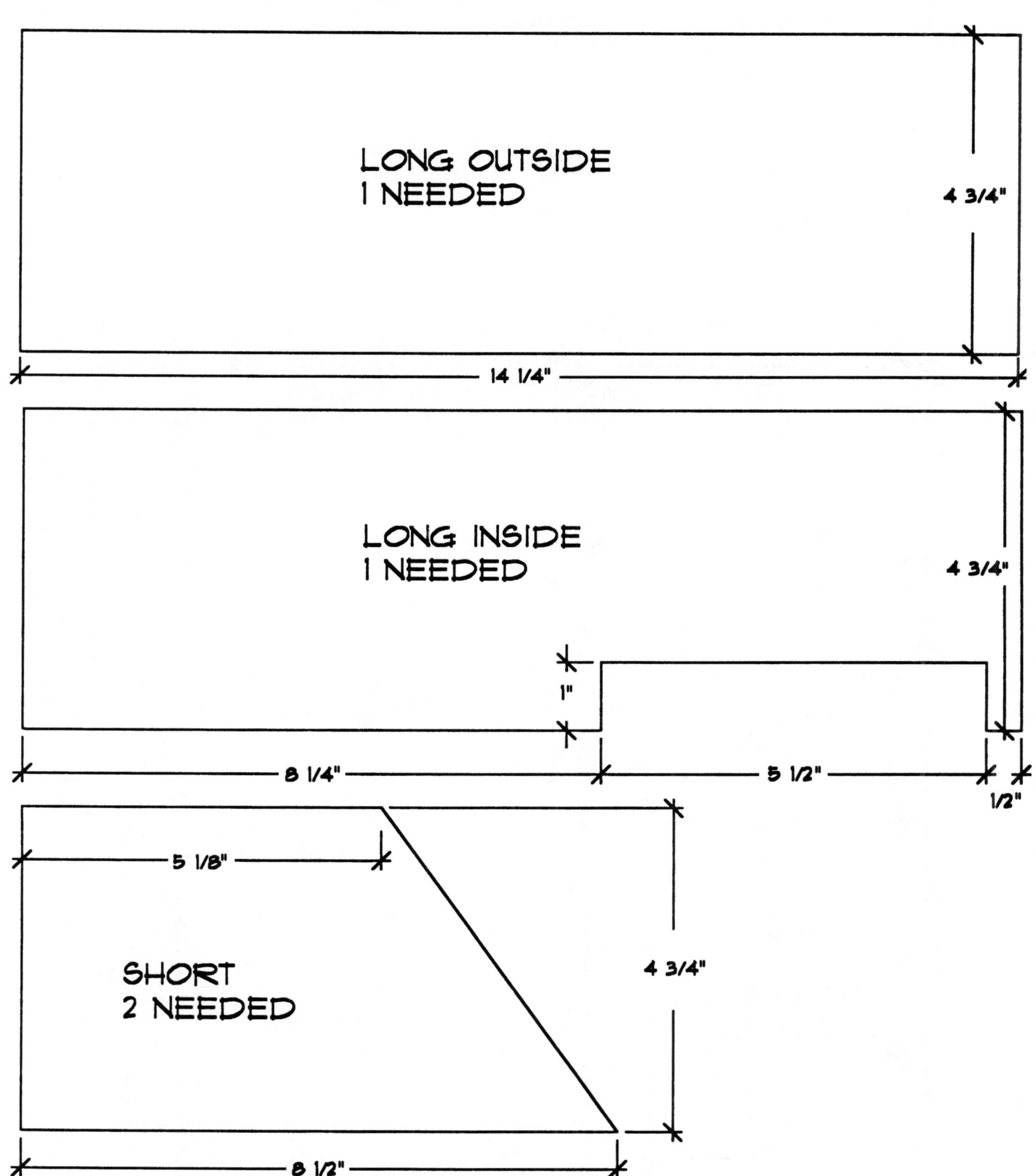

This design is based on cabins I have visited near the lakes and ski areas of the Pocono Mountains.

For the most part, this is a purely functional birdhouse. The only decorative stuff — the skylight and flowers — can be eliminated if you want. The Pocono is designed for chickadees, but can be adapted for just about any bird.

I used redwood and left it natural. I also found some 1/2" redwood stock which I used for the roof. My plans here call for 3/4" redwood all around.

Materials list:

(1) 6-foot 1 x 6 board

4d galvanized finish nails

(4) #8 1-1/2" brass wood screws (to attach bottom)

Type II weatherproof glue

3" x 9" strip of 36-gauge copper tooling foil (optional – for roof peak)

7/16" solid copper tacks (optional – to make flowers)

Assorted small galvanized or aluminum common nails (optional – to make flowers)

Common window glass (optional – to make skylight)

Silicone sealant (optional – for skylight)

Instructions:

For instructions on how this birdhouse is built, refer to the *Building Basics* section.

What is not covered in *Building Basics* is how to make the optional flowers, skylights and copper roof peak.

1. To make flowers, bend aluminum or galvanized common nails to look like droopy flowers. Paint each flower. Drill holes in the top of the entrance hole block just large enough to hold the nail flowers. Paint each flower, then insert the flower into a hole with a tiny drop of glue to hold it.

2. To make the skylights, draw an outline of each piece of skylight glass or plastic on each roof panel BEFORE THE ROOF IS INSTALLED. Make sure you leave room at the top of the roof peak to accommodate the overlap you will have with this roof.

Use a chisel to cut around the outline to a depth equal to the thickness of the glass or other material you will be using for the skylight.

Cut out a hole slightly smaller than the skylight material using a drill and coping saw. Use a chisel to cut a ledge around the inside of the hole.

AFTER THE ROOF IS IN PLACE AND ALL THE NAILING IS DONE (INCLUDING THE COPPER ROOF PEAK, IF ANY), put a small bead of silicone sealant around the hole for the skylight and set it in place.

3. To make the copper roof peak, place your copper strip over the peak of the roof and nail it in place using solid copper tacks. Do this before putting in the skylight material. At each end of the roof peak, you can bend the remaining copper down over the front and back, overlap it, and attach it with one copper tack.

POCONO

ENDS (2 NEEDED-ACCESS HOLE IN ONE)
SIDES (2 NEEDED)
1 X 6

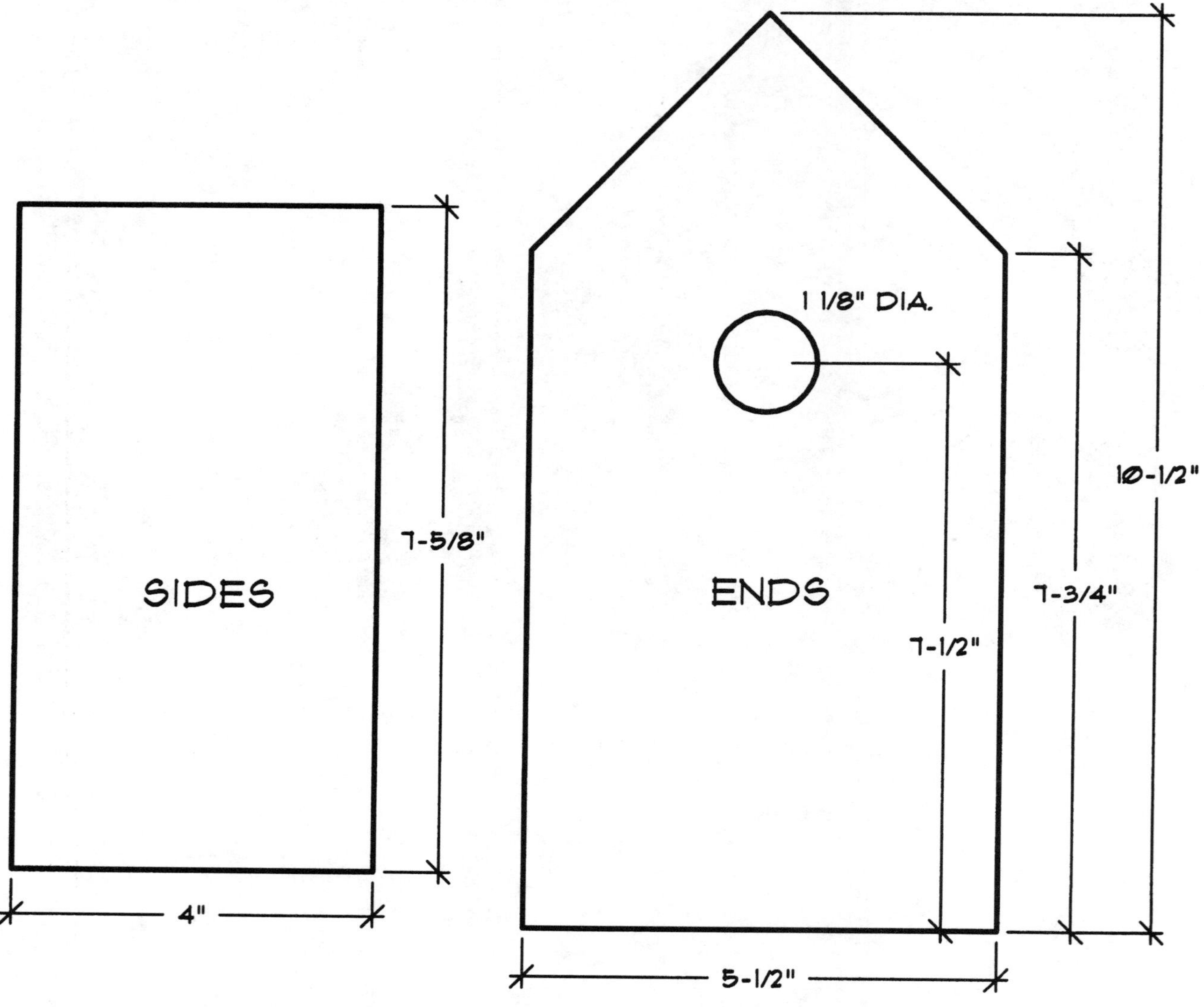

POCONO
ROOF PIECES, BOTTOM & PREDATOR GUARD
1 X 6

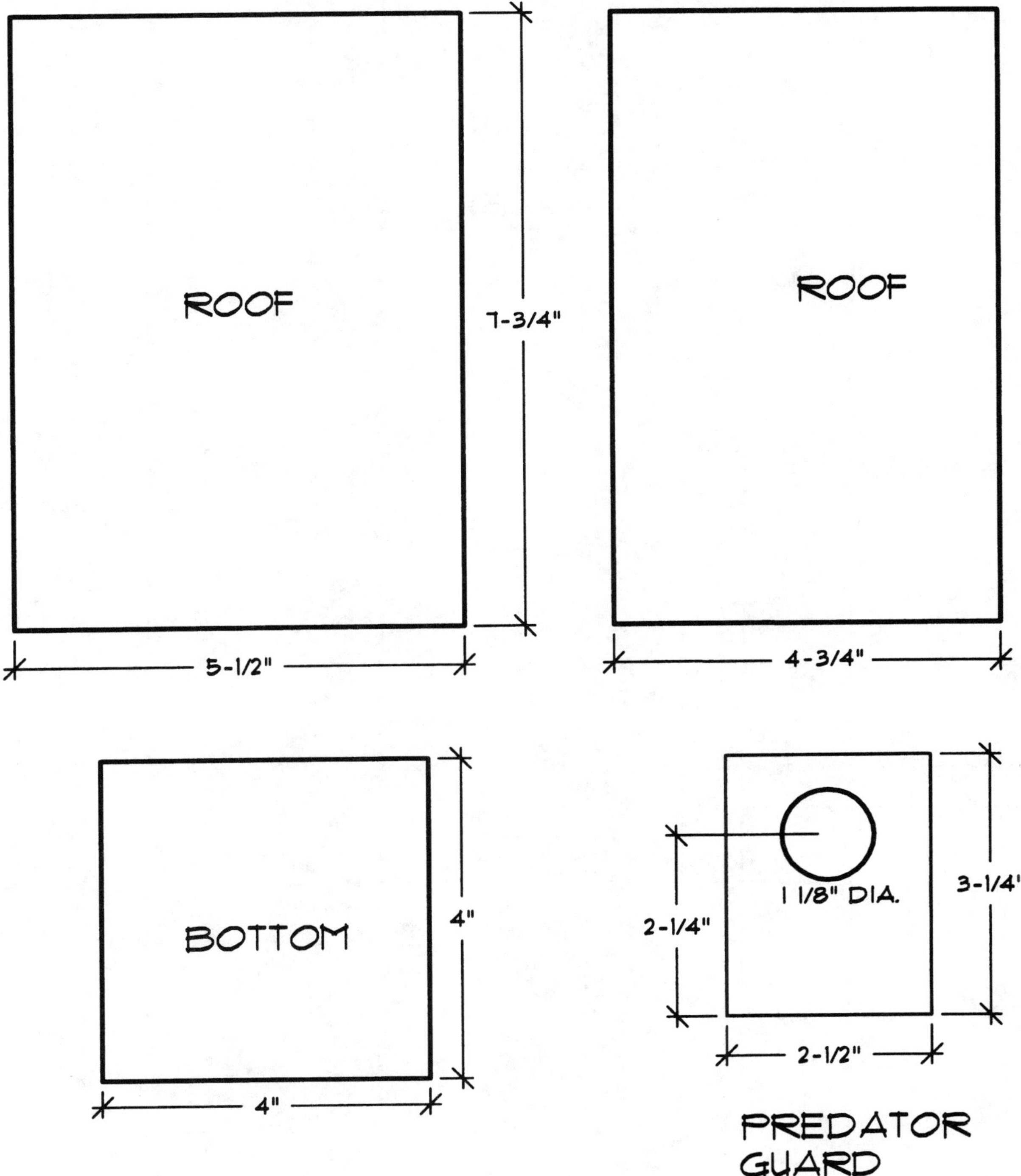

Malcolm Wells' Fence Board House.

Architect Malcolm Wells has designed some very exciting and refreshing birdhouses and feeders during the past 40 years. 25 of these designs are in his book ***Classic Architectural Birdhouses and Feeders.***

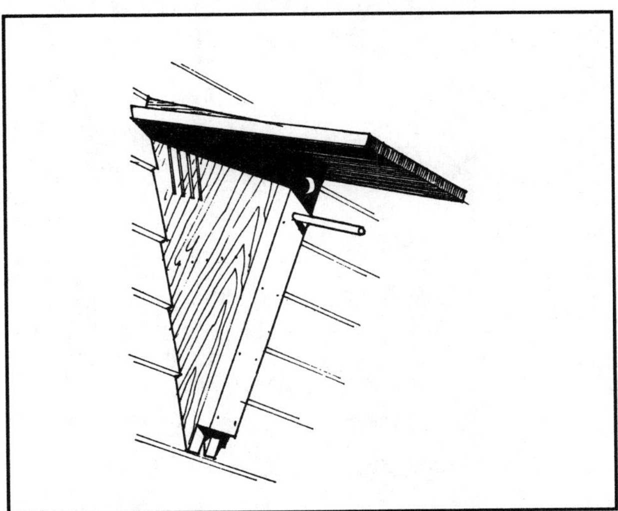

The Wedge.

The Hangout.

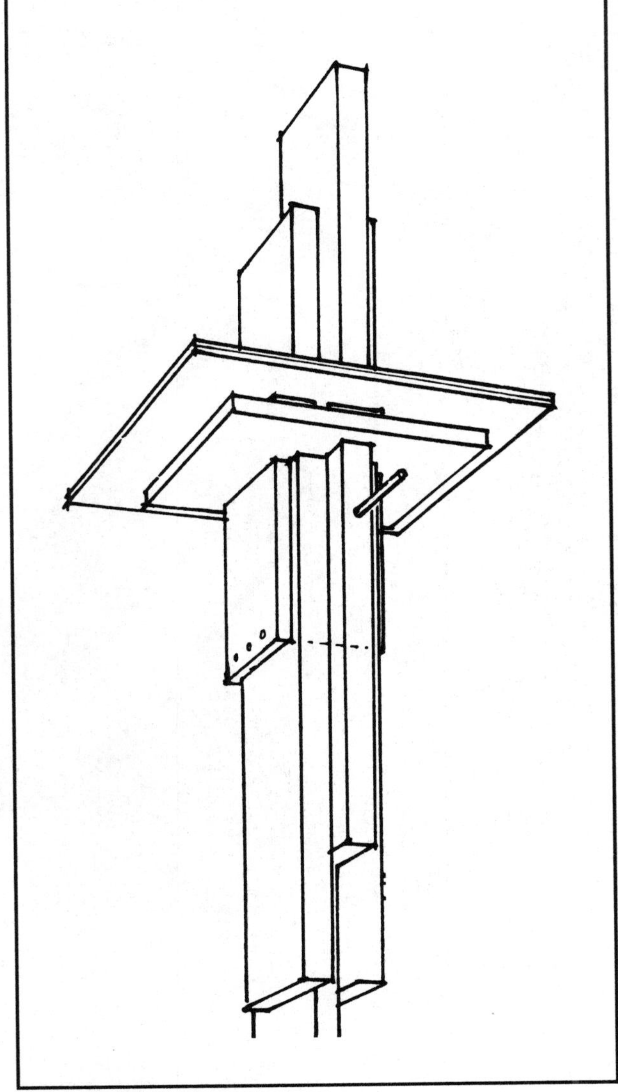

The Skyscraper.

The Hangout

Wait!
Don't turn the page. It isn't as hard as it looks. And it doesn't look as complicated as you think. After you've looked at it a while you'll see that it's not confusing or complicated; it's simply unified.
If you're going to say "45 degrees" in a design, you don't want to do it hesitantly or everyone will be embarrassed. Say it with strength, and then carry it through into the details. It's what nature does with all the details. Look at any flower, any pine cone, any leaf. This is just a poor attempt to go all-out the way the living world does.

This is a simple 45° birdhouse with a few modifications.

First, I pulled one side down, then I elongated the roof on that side.

Next, I added a center fin, or vane, to act as a wall bracket.

Following that, I made the entrance square and added a strip below the entrance to echo the roof angle.

Then it was just a matter of perches and details.

That doesn't sound very bad, now, does it?

Even the square perches are easy. Simply carve their ends using a utility knife, and force them into the holes you've drilled.

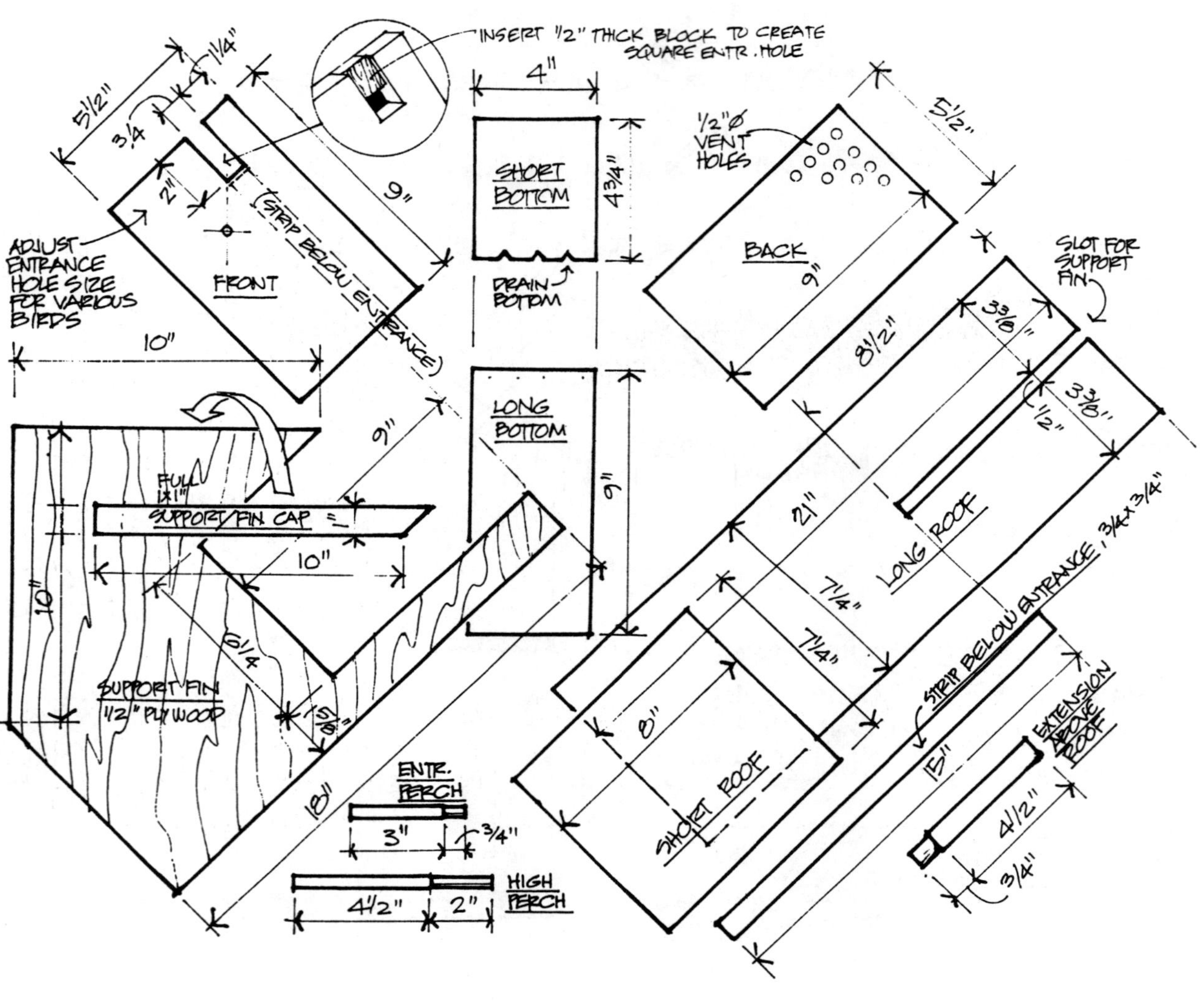

INSERT 1/2" THICK BLOCK TO CREATE SQUARE ENTR. HOLE
5 1/2"
5 1/4"
3/4"
2"
9"
FRONT
(STRIP BELOW ENTRANCE)
ADJUST ENTRANCE HOLE SIZE FOR VARIOUS BIRDS
10"
4"
SHORT BOTTOM
4 3/4"
DRAIN BOTTOM
1/2" Ø VENT HOLES
BACK
9"
5 1/2"
SLOT FOR SUPPORT FIN
8 1/2"
3 3/8"
3 3/8"
1/2"
LONG ROOF
9"
LONG BOTTOM
9"
FULL 1 x 1"
SUPPORT FIN CAP
10"
10"
10 1/4"
1 1/2"
SUPPORT FIN 1/2" PLYWOOD
18"
21"
7 1/4"
7 1/4"
STRIP BELOW ENTRANCE 3/4 x 3/4"
8"
SHORT ROOF
ENTR. PERCH
3"
3/4"
HIGH PERCH
4 1/2"
2"
15"
EXTENSION ABOVE ROOF
4 1/2"
3/4"

The Wedge

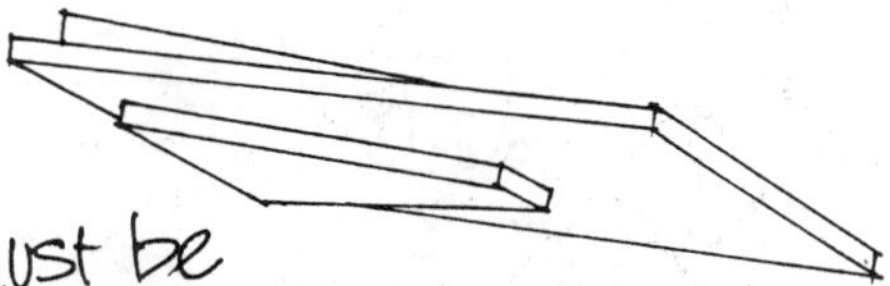

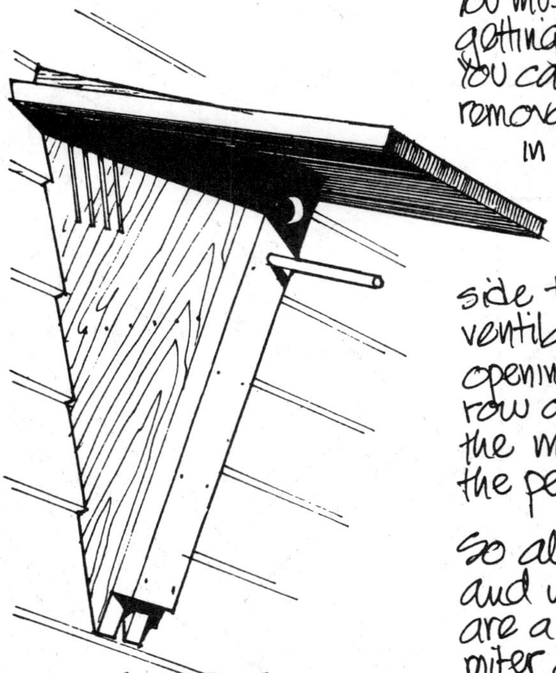

You must be
getting pretty good at all this by now.
You can tell at a glance, I'll bet, that the
removable roof of this birdhouse is held
in place by 1) the weight of the 2" thick
board atop the roof, plus 2) the
3/4" board on the underside
that's cut to fit snugly inside the walls. You've noticed the 4
ventilation slots on each side, the drain
opening at the bottom, the horizontal
row of nails locating the floor, and
the matching slopes of the roof and
the perch.

So all you need are a few dimensions
and you'll be on your way. The shapes
are a little tricky but unless you try to
miter all the odd-angle joints you

REMEMBER THE TABLE
ON PAGE 17! HOLE SIZE
AND MOUNTING HEIGHT
DETERMINE TYPE OF OCCUPANT.

should have no trouble.
Now I will cross my
fingers and hope that
the dimensions are
right. If they
aren't, well,
I can offer
you a
refund on
the book, or
you could shave
a bit here and
cut a bit there until it
all goes together.

Remember that no matter
how proud you are to have
made this birdhouse, Mother

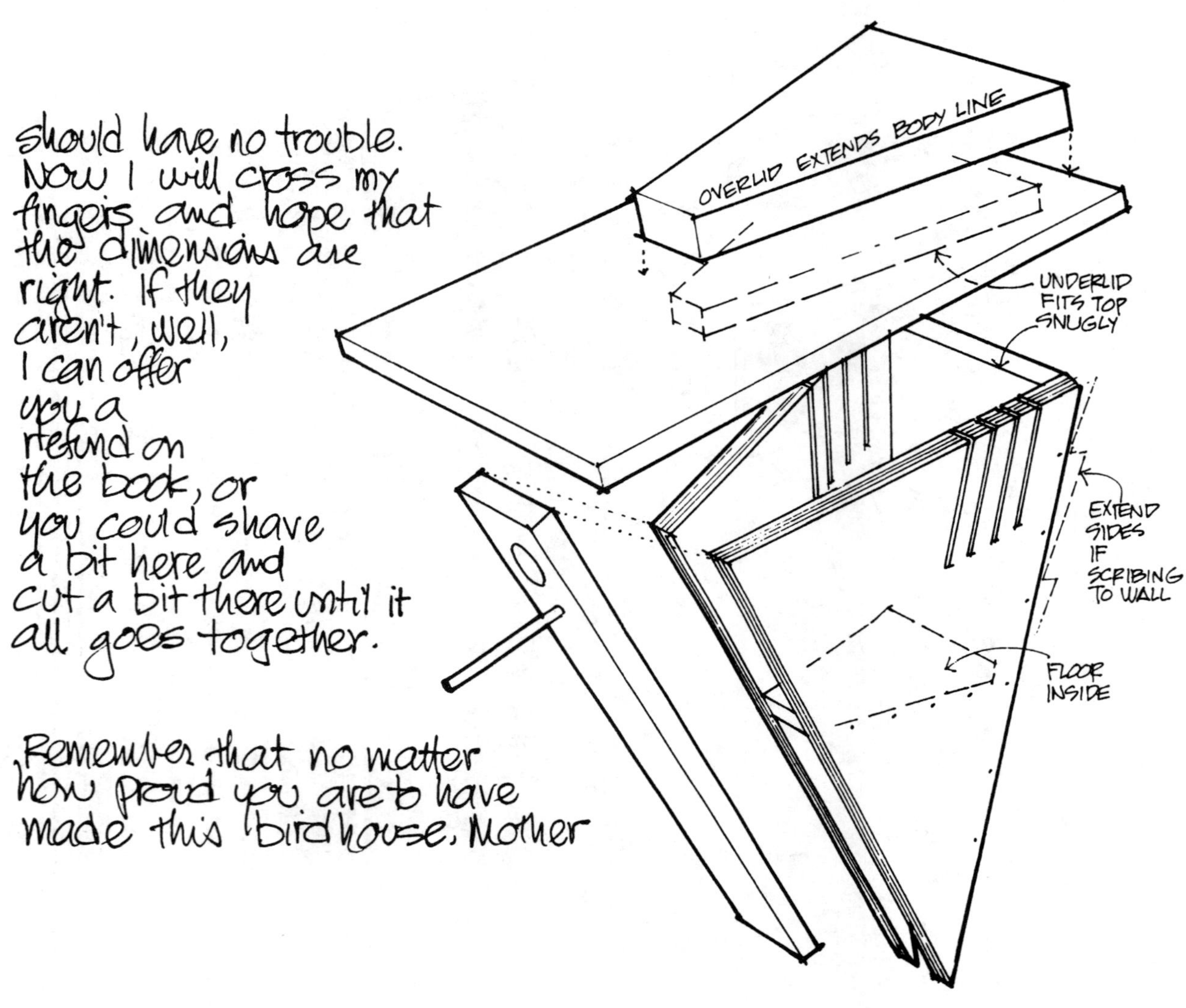

Nature will want you to hide it among the leaves (where it and all man-made things belong).

This cross section is shown as if it were mounted against a flat wall. If the wall is not flat — if it is shingled or if it has beveled siding, all you need do, after you're 100% sure where you want to hang it, is to scribe and cut the overhanging side pieces as shown at left. This can be done after the birdhouse has been assembled.

Now, on to the cutting.....

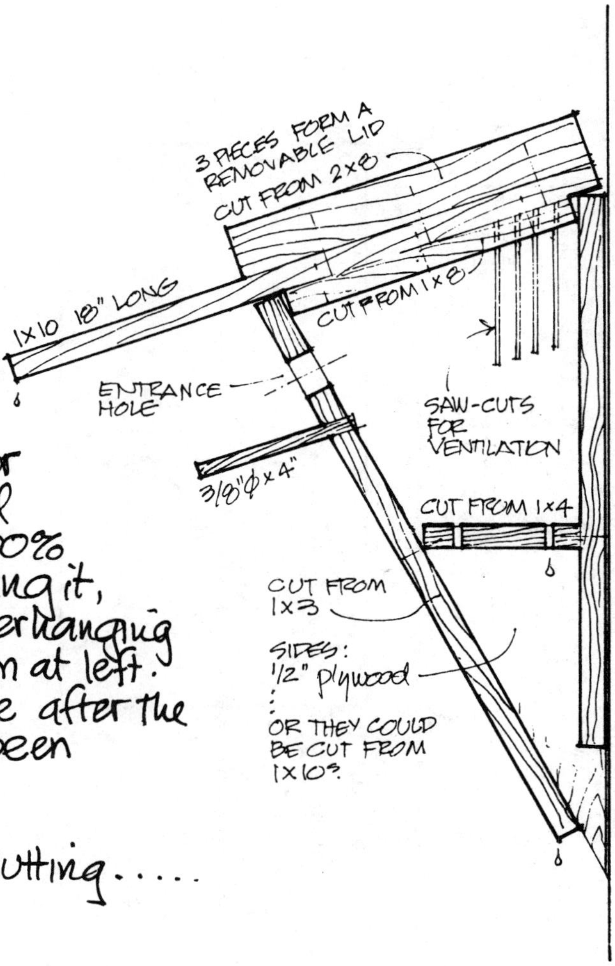

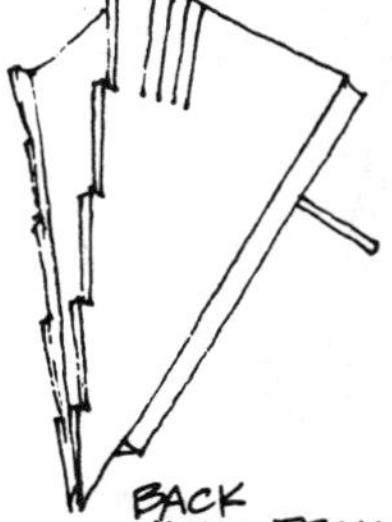

Needed: <u>one</u> of each piece, except the 2 side pieces.

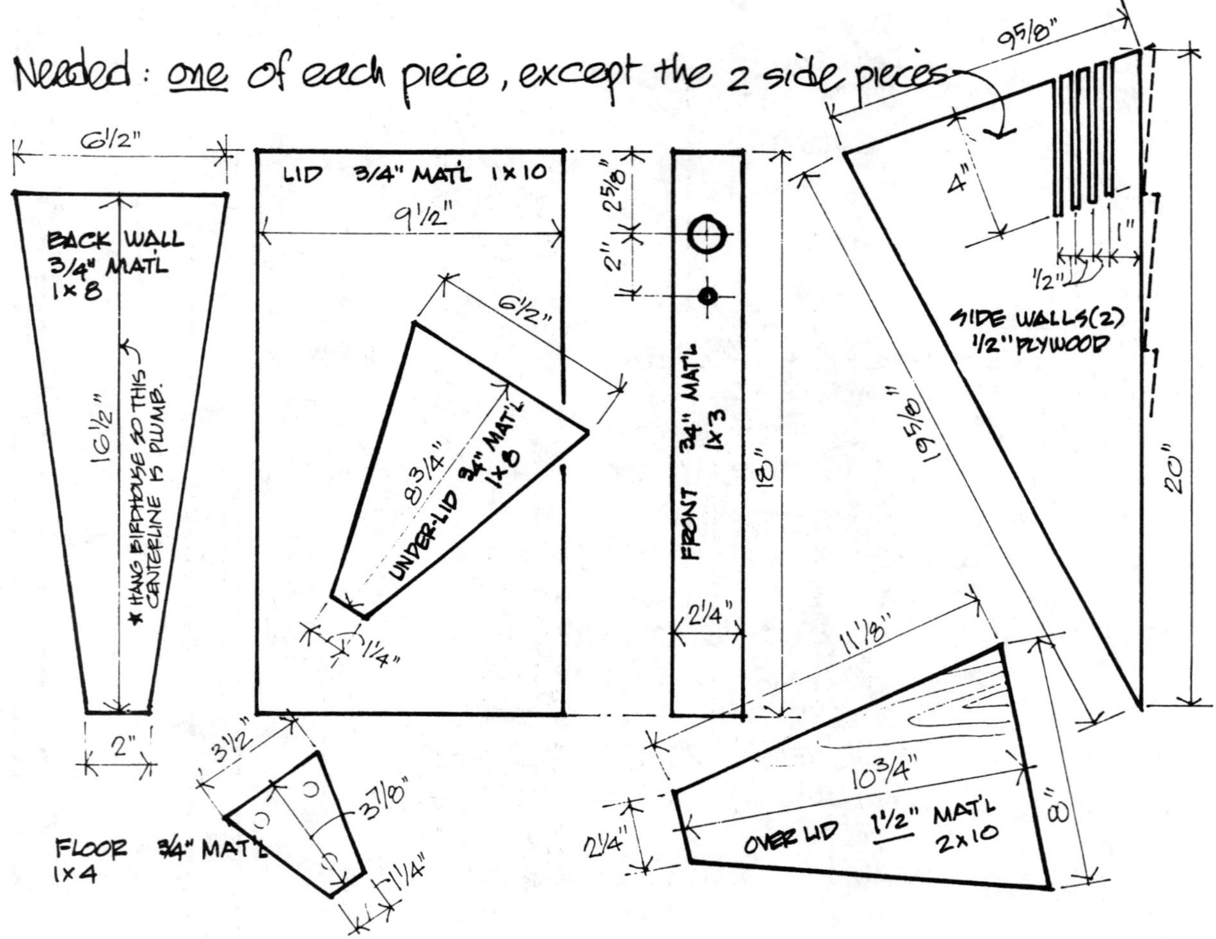

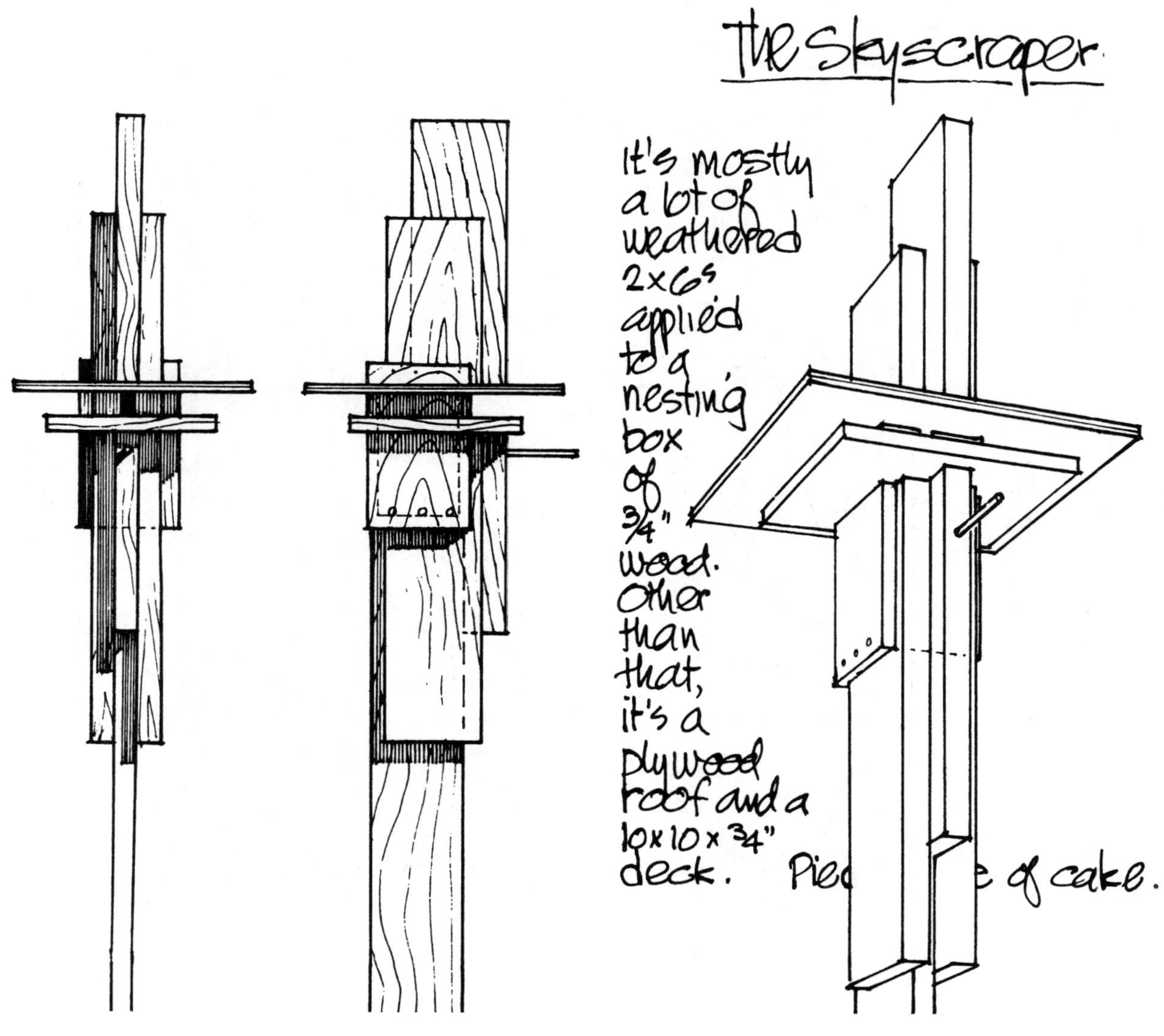
The Skyscraper.
It's mostly a lot of weathered 2×6s applied to a nesting box of 3/4" wood. Other than that, it's a plywood roof and a 10×10×3/4" deck. Piece of cake.

I mean, if you've got to go for height, <u>emphasize</u> it. Stress the vertical.

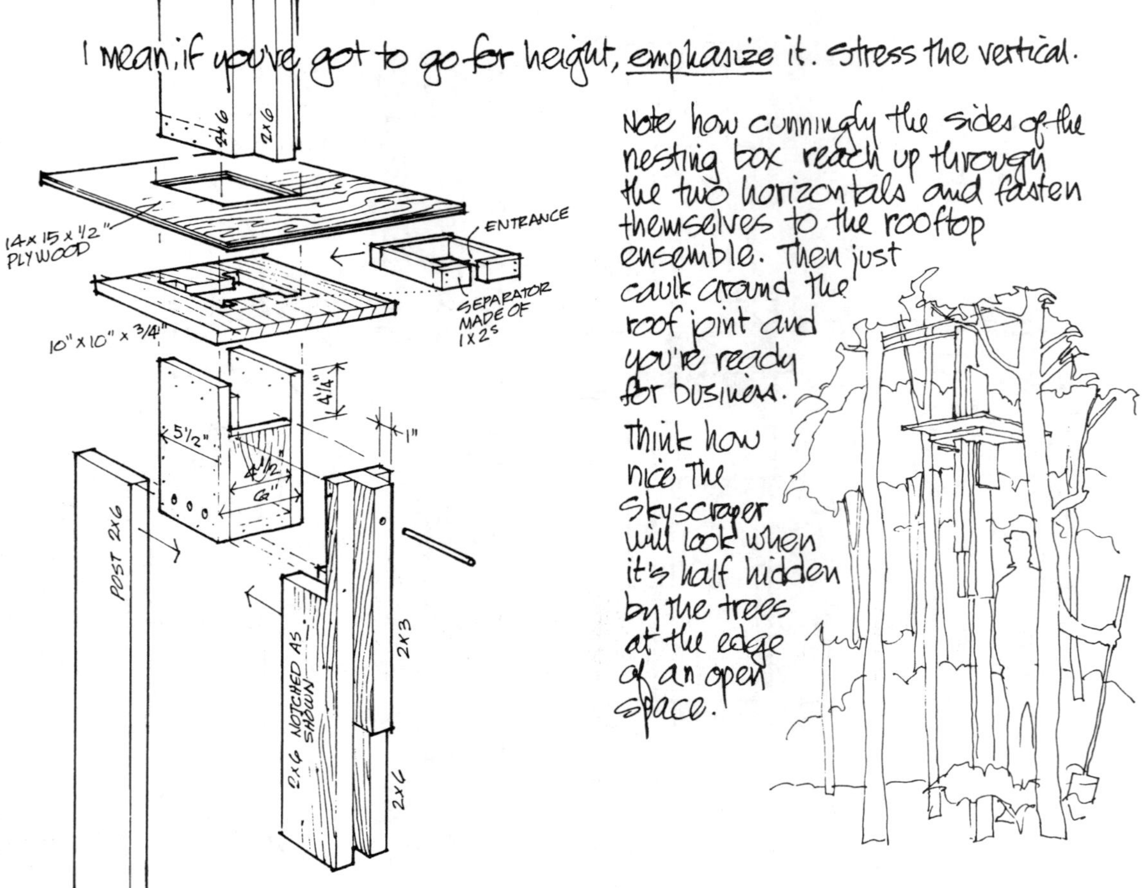

Note how cunningly the sides of the nesting box reach up through the two horizontals and fasten themselves to the rooftop ensemble. Then just caulk around the roof joint and you're ready for business.

Think how nice the skyscraper will look when it's half hidden by the trees at the edge of an open space.

These plans are at over 70 years old and reflect the architectural styles and practical design elements of their time.

One element you'll see recurring in these plans is the platform floor. Practical experience over the years has shown birdhouse builders that platform floors tend to allow water to wick into the walls and nesting area of the birdhouse.

You may want to modify these plans to replace the platform floor with a recessed floor. To achieve the same visual effect as a platform floor, extend the walls 3/4" lower than the plans call for, then attach pieces of 3/4" thick lumber to the walls around the outside of the house, flush with the bottom of the house. Drill small drainage holes next to the walls so water doesn't collect there.

Some of these birdhouses may not provide the amount of ventilation required by today's standards. It's easy to add ventilation. A few holes drilled in areas protected from rain should be sufficient

CORNER WREN HOUSE

BILL OF MATERIAL

2 PC   ½" x 7¾" x 7¾" x 11"   TOP & BOTTOM

1 PC   ½" x 5½" x 8"   BACK

1 PC   ½" x 6" x 8"   "

1 PC   ½" x 9½" x 8"   FRONT

2 PC   11"   COVE MOLD

1 PC   ¼" x 2¼" ROUND PERCH

6   ½" SCREWS

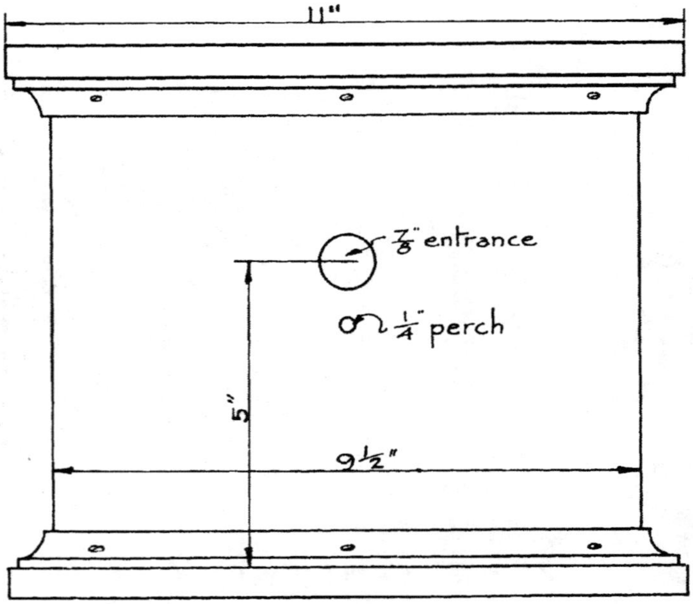

FRONT VIEW

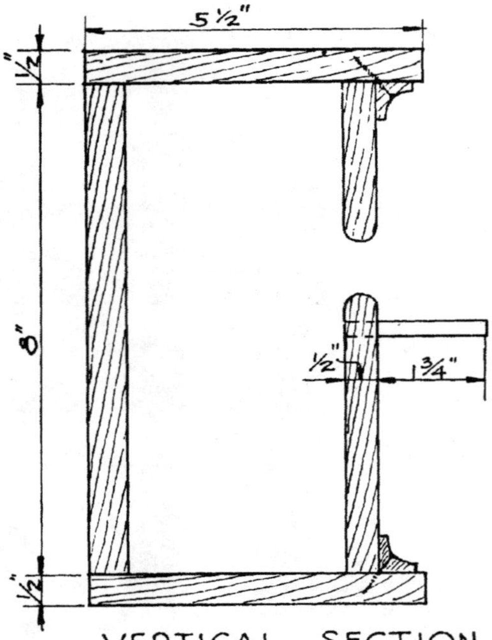

VERTICAL SECTION

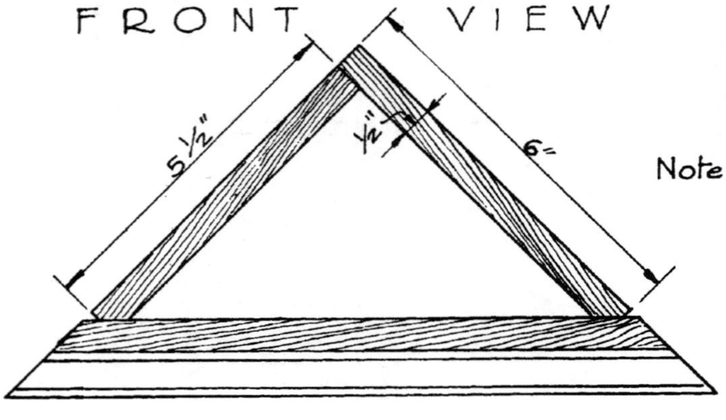

PLAN

Note: Remove front for cleaning.

BUNGALOW

WREN HOUSE

BILL OF MATERIAL.

1 PC	3/8" x 6" x 9½"		BOTTOM
1 PC	3/8" x 1⅝" x 6½"		PORCH FLOOR
1 PC	3/8" x 2⅛" x 3¼"		" "
2 PC	3/8" x 4" x 5½"		ENDS
1 PC	3/8" x 6¼" x 4"		FRONT
1 PC	3/8" x 6¼" x 2¾"		DRAWER
1 PC	3/8" x 6¼" x 1"		BACK
1 PC	¼" x 3⅝" x 6¼"		DRAWER BOTTOM
1 PC	3/8" x 4" x 7"		FRONT PORCH ROOF
4 PC	3/8" x 3/8" x 2"	" "	POSTS
1 PC	3/8" x ¾" x 6¼"	" "	BEAM
2 PC	3/8" x ¾" x 1¼"	" "	"
2 PC	3/8" x 1" x 2⅛"	SIDE "	
2 PC	3/8" x 3/8" x 1⅜"	" "	POSTS
2 PC	3/8" x ¾" x 1¾"	" "	BEAM
1 PC	3/8" x ¾" x 3¼"	" "	"
2 PC	¼" x ½" x 1¾"	" "	RAIL
2 PC	¾" x 3¾" x 8½"		ROOF
1 PC	3/8" x 3½" x 4"		DORMER ROOF
1 PC	3/8" x 3¼" x 2¼"	"	FRONT
2 PC	3/8" x 2½" x 1¾"	"	SIDES
2 PC	¾" x 1" x 1½"		CHIMNEY
2 PC	¼" x 1" x 1¼"	"	CAP

OYSTER SHELLS ON FRESH PAINT FOR STUCCO

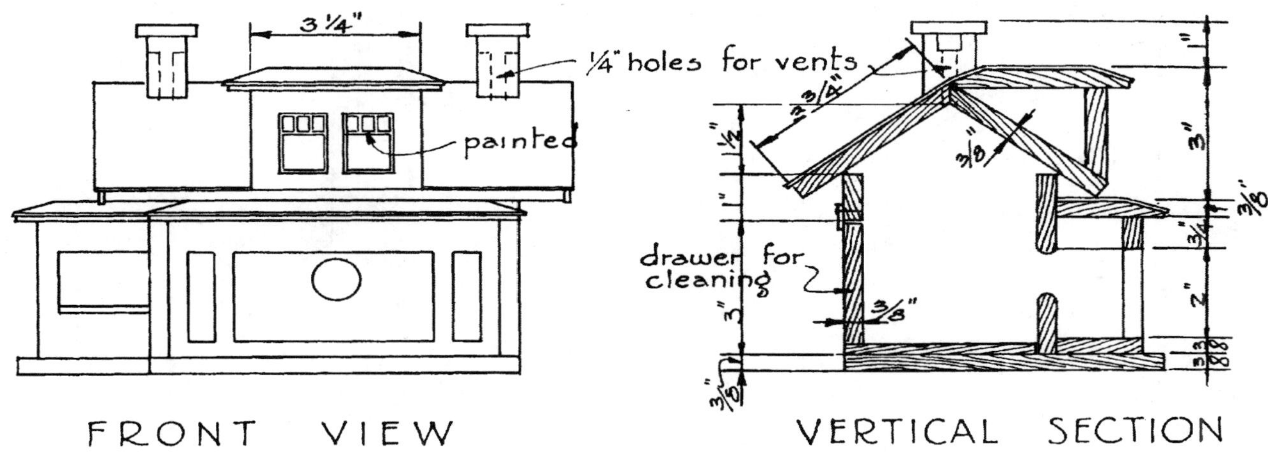

FRONT VIEW

VERTICAL SECTION

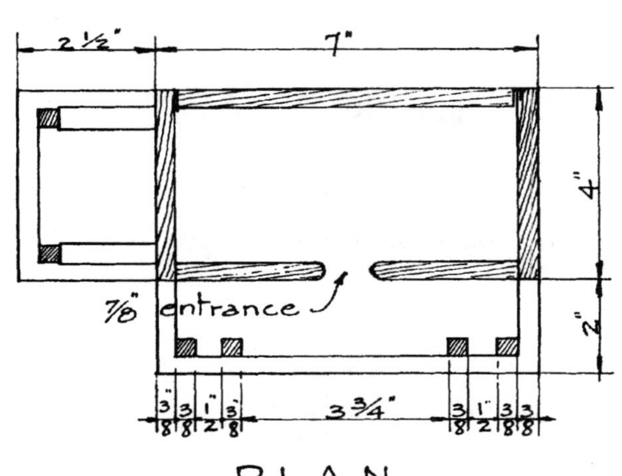

PLAN

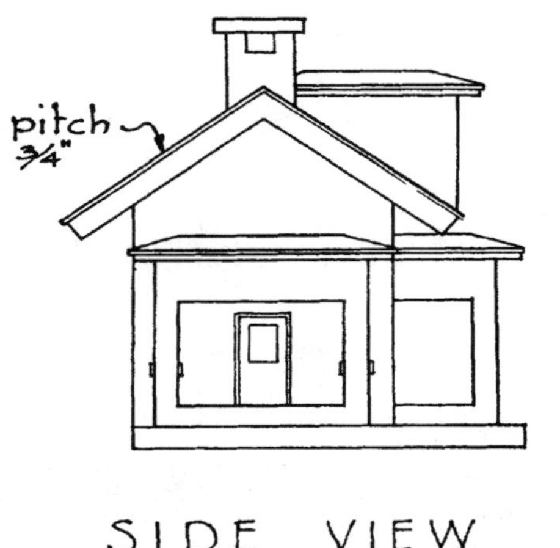

SIDE VIEW

SUMMER HOME FOR JENNY WREN

BILL OF MATERIAL

1	PC	3/4" × 5 3/4" × 5 3/4"	BOTTOM
4	PC	1/2" × 3/4" × 3"	SILLS
2	PC	1/2" × 3/4" × 3"	PLATE
4	PC	3/4" × 3/4" × 5"	POSTS
2	PC	3/4" × 4 1/2" × 2"	GABLES
1	PC	3/8" × 4" × 5 1/2"	ROOF
1	PC	3/8" × 4 1/2" × 5 1/2"	"
1	PC	3/8" × 1 1/4" × 4"	HANGER
1	PC	5" × 19"	SCREEN
4		1 1/2" SCREWS # 10	

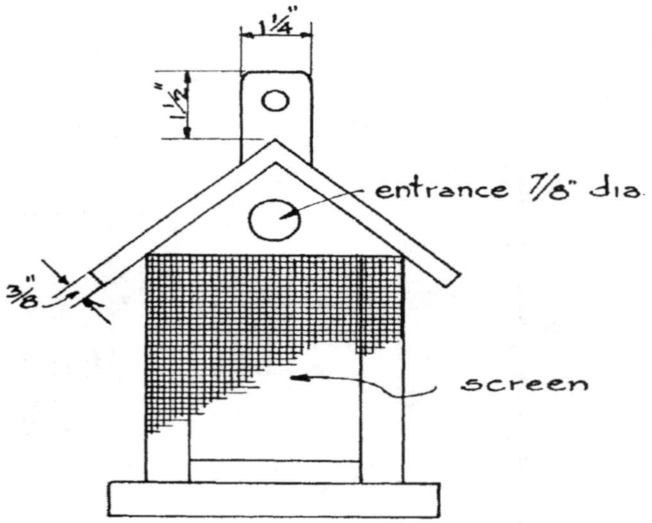

FRONT VIEW

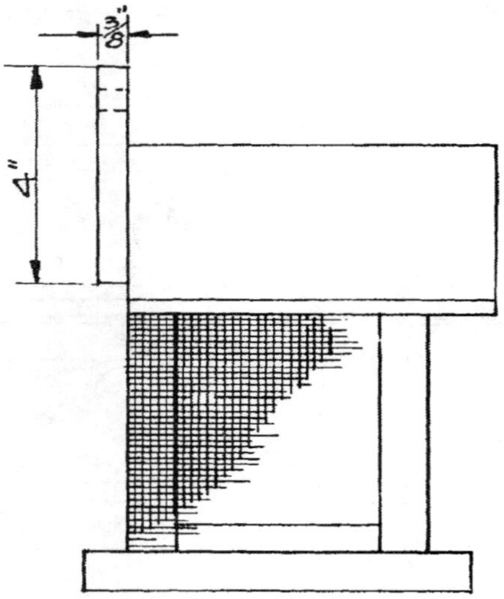

SIDE VIEW

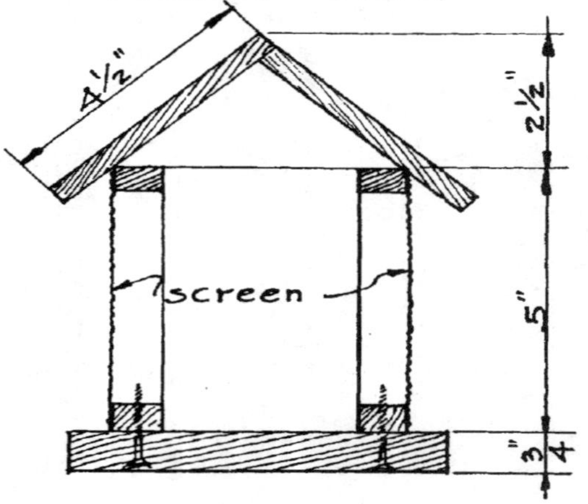

SECTION

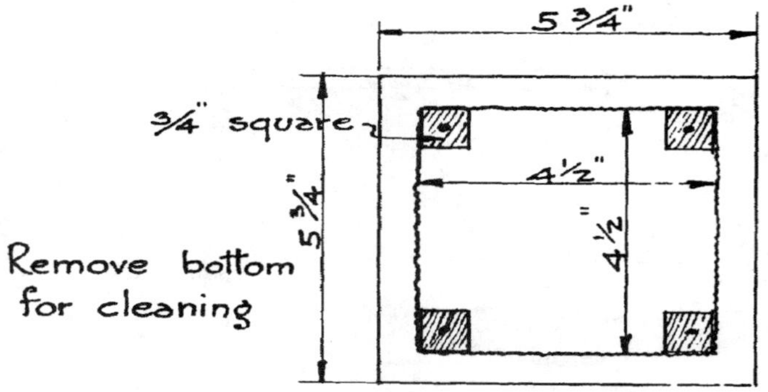

PLAN

Remove bottom for cleaning

Note: A wren house built on this plan has been occupied for five seasons.

ENGLISH COTTAGE

2 ROOM BLUEBIRD HOUSE
BILL OF MATERIAL

1	PC	3/4" x 8" x 14"	BOTTOM
1	PC	3/4" x 1 1/2" x 4 1/4"	PORCH FLOOR
1	PC	3/8" x 11 1/8" x 6"	BACK
1	PC	3/8" x 11 1/8" x 7 3/4"	FRONT
2	PC	3/8" x 6" x 6"	ENDS
1	PC	3/8" x 6" x 10"	PARTITIONS
2	PC	3/8" x 11 1/8" x 5 1/2"	ROOF
2	PC	3/8" x 6" x 4 3/8"	"
1	PC	3/8" x 1 1/2" x 3"	PORCH
2	PC	3/8" x 3/8" x 2"	" COLUMN
1	PC	3/4" x 1 1/2" x 3"	" ROOF
2	PC	1/4" x 2 1/2" x 1"	PERCH
2	PC	3/4" x 2 1/2" x 1 1/4"	CHIMNEYS
2	PC	1/4" QUARTER RD.	PERCH
1	PAIR HINGES		
1	HOOK		

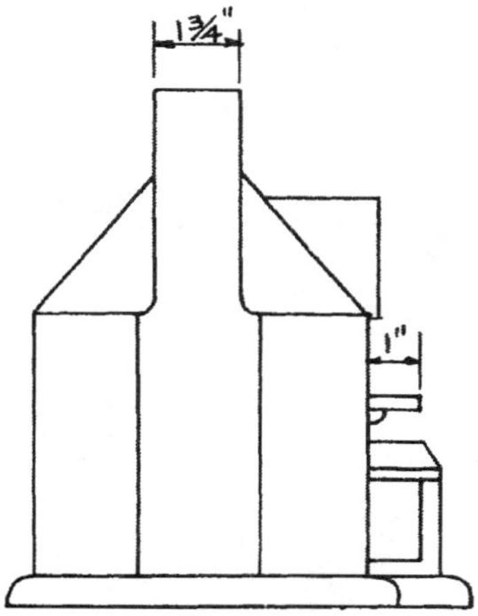

SIDE VIEW

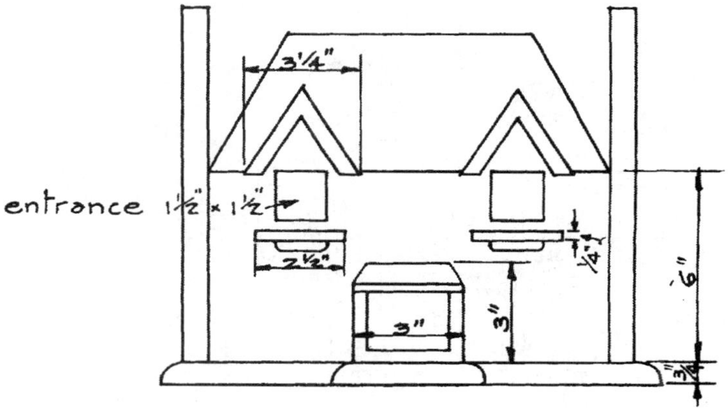

FRONT VIEW

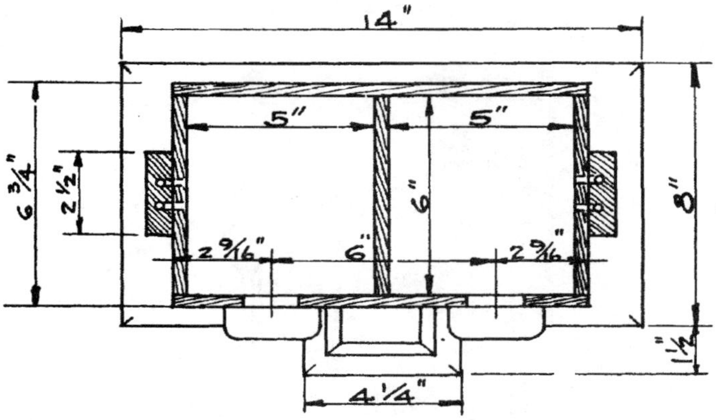

PLAN

Note Bottom hinged for cleaning.

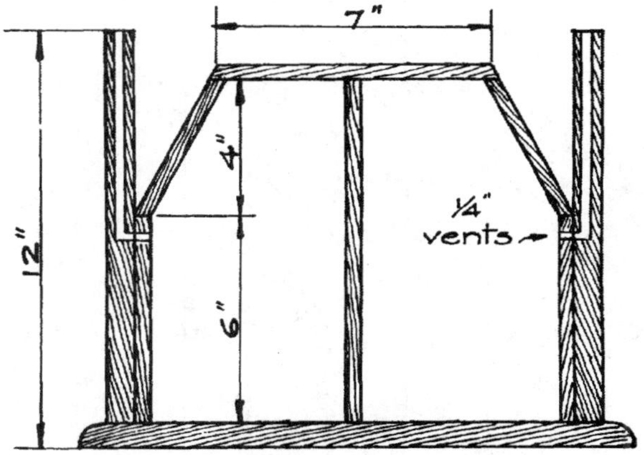

SECTION

JAPANESE BLUEBIRD

THIS HOUSE WON SECOND
PRIZE IN A BIRDHOUSE CONTEST

BILL OF MATERIAL

6 PC ½" x 5" to 3½" x 9½" SIDES
6 PC ½" x 5" to 2" x 4½" "
1 PC ¾" x 4" HEXAGON TOP
1 PC ¾" x 2" " "
1 PC ¾" x 7" " BOTTOM
130" ¼" x ⅜" STRIP
360" HALF ROUND "
1 PC 7" BENT TWIG PERCH
1 HOOK

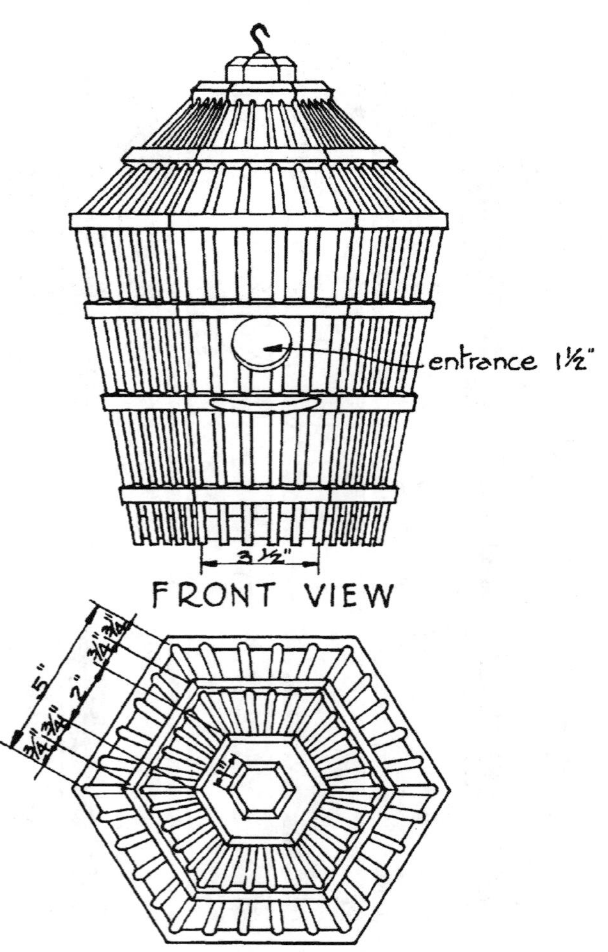

FRONT VIEW

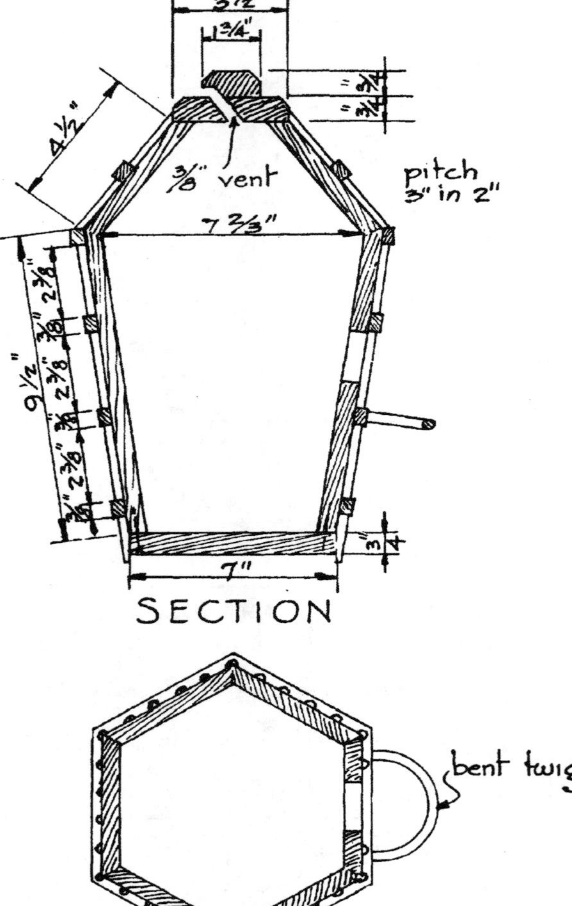

SECTION

TOP VIEW

PLAN

Note: Bottom comes off for cleaning

THE "CLOCK"

TWO ROOM WREN HOUSE
BILL OF MATERIAL

1 PC	½" × 4" × 9½"	BOTTOM
2 PC	½" × 11½" × 9"	FRONT & BACK
2 PC	½" × 4" × 5"	SIDES
1 PC	½" × 4" × 7½"	PARTITION
2 PC	½" × 6½" × 7½"	ROOF
2 PC	¼" ROUND × 2½"	PERCH
1 PC	½" × 1" × 6"	HANGER
2	TIN CLOCK HANDS	
1	HINGE	
1	HOOK	
2	PINE CONES	
7"	SASH CHAIN	

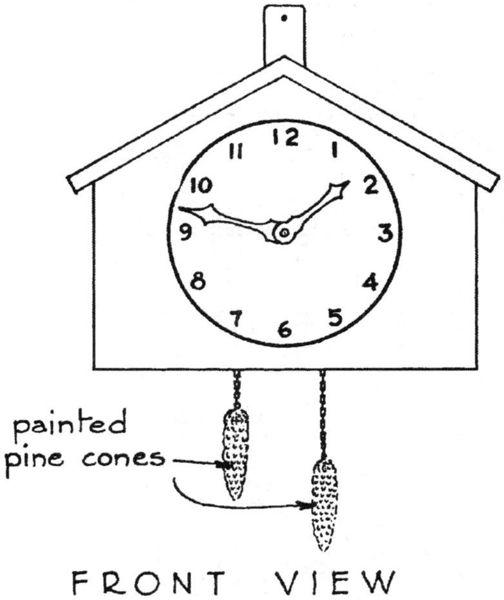

FRONT VIEW

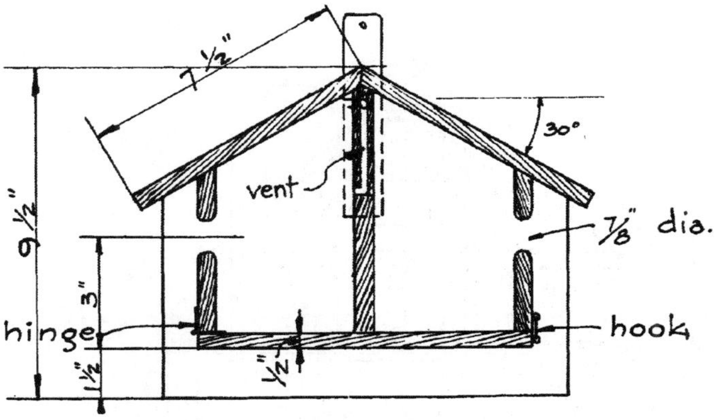

painted pine cones

VERTICAL SECTION

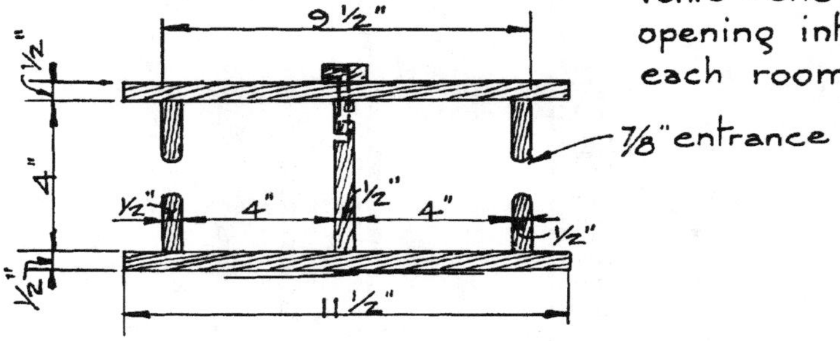

7½"
30°
vent
9½"
3"
1½"
½"
hinge
hook
⅞" dia.

PLAN

9½"
½"
4"
½"
4"
½"
4"
½"
11½"
⅞" entrance

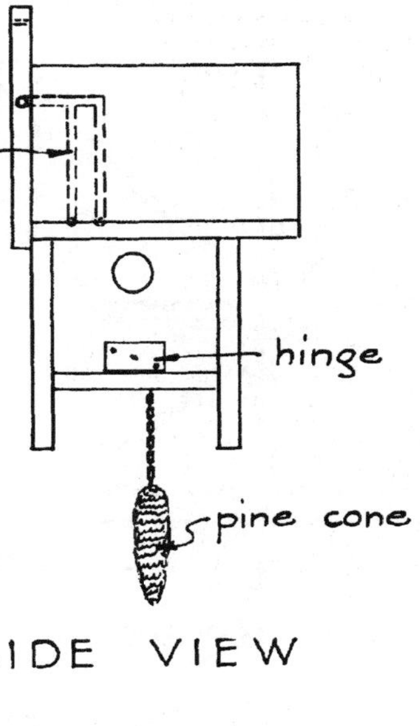

SIDE VIEW

¼" holes for vents - one opening into each room

hinge

pine cone

THE RESIDENCE

18 ROOM MARTIN HOUSE

BILL OF MATERIAL

Qty		Dimensions	Description
1	PC	3/4" x 26" x 27"	BOTTOM
4	PC	1/2" x 13" x 18"	SIDES
2	PC	1/2" x 4" x 19"	PORCH FLOOR
2	PC	1/2" x 4" x 26"	" "
16	PC	1/2" x 1/2" x 4 1/2"	" COLUMNS
4	PC	1/2" x 1" x 26"	" BEAM
2	PC	1/2" x 4" x 26"	" ROOF
2	PC	1/2" x 4" x 27	" "
4	PC	1/2" x 8 3/4" x 17"	2nd & 3rd FLOORS
4	PC	1/2" x 8 1/4" x 6"	PARTITIONS
8	PC	1/2" x 12" x 6"	"
4	PC	1/2" x 17" x 6"	"
2	PC	1/2" x 1" x 13"	" STRIPS
2	PC	1/2" x 4" x 16"	EAVES
2	PC	1/2" x 4" x 23"	"
2	PC	1/2" x 15" x 23"	ROOF
2	PC	1/2 x 15" x 24"	"
1	PC	1/2 x 9" x 20"	PARTITION
2	PC	1/2 x 4 1/2" x 3"	DORMER FRONTS
4	PC	1/2" x 3" x 2 1/2"	" SIDES
2	PC	1/2" x 6 1/2" x 5"	" CEILING
2	PC	1/2" x 6 1/2" x 3 1/2"	" ROOF
4	PC	1/2" x 8" x 4"	" "
12	PC	1/2" x 2" x 2"	BRACKETS
2	PC	1/2" x 2" x 10"	CHIMNEY
2	PC	1/2" x 2" x 9"	"
1	PC	1/2" x 2 1/4 x 8 1/4"	" CAP

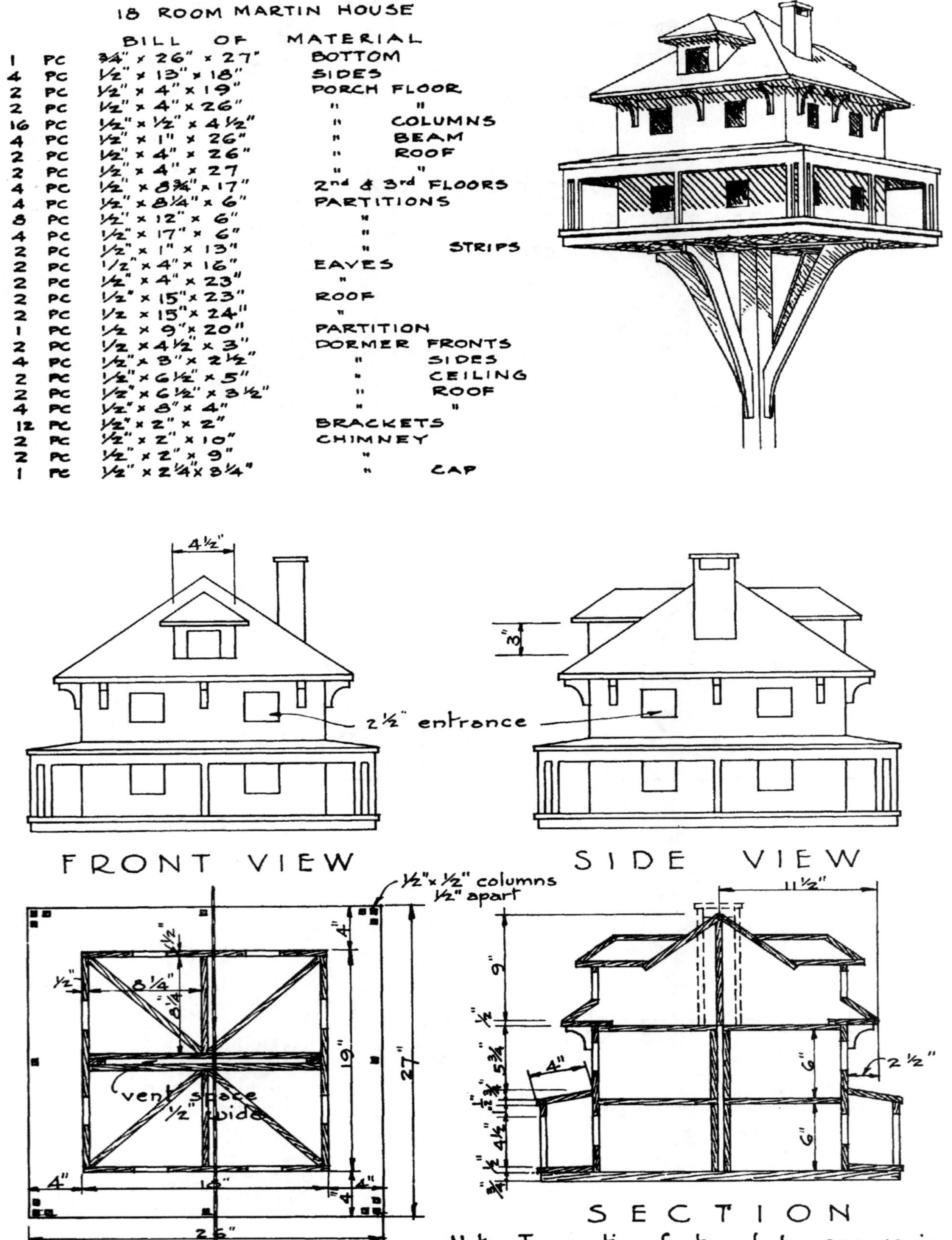

Note: Top section fastened by screws in brackets. 1st & 2nd floors & partitions built in unit and lift out for cleaning.

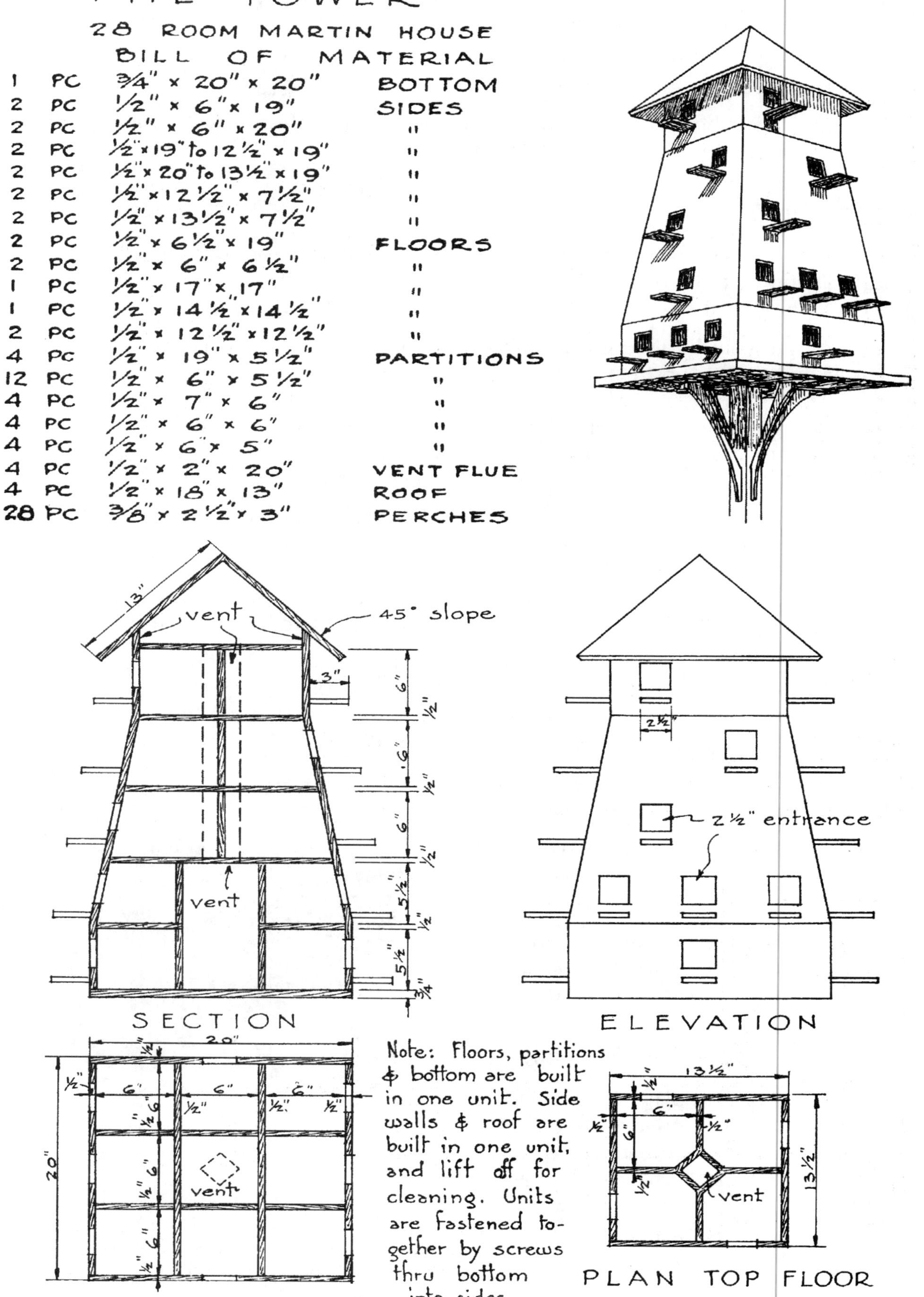

THE TOWER
28 ROOM MARTIN HOUSE
BILL OF MATERIAL
1 PC 3/4" x 20" x 20" BOTTOM
2 PC 1/2" x 6" x 19" SIDES
2 PC 1/2" x 6" x 20" "
2 PC 1/2" x 19" to 12 1/2" x 19" "
2 PC 1/2" x 20" to 13 1/2" x 19" "
2 PC 1/2" x 12 1/2" x 7 1/2" "
2 PC 1/2" x 13 1/2" x 7 1/2" "
2 PC 1/2" x 6 1/2" x 19" FLOORS
2 PC 1/2" x 6" x 6 1/2" "
1 PC 1/2" x 17" x 17" "
1 PC 1/2" x 14 1/2" x 14 1/2" "
2 PC 1/2" x 12 1/2" x 12 1/2" "
4 PC 1/2" x 19" x 5 1/2" PARTITIONS
12 PC 1/2" x 6" x 5 1/2" "
4 PC 1/2" x 7" x 6" "
4 PC 1/2" x 6" x 6" "
4 PC 1/2" x 6" x 5" "
4 PC 1/2" x 2" x 20" VENT FLUE
4 PC 1/2" x 18" x 13" ROOF
28 PC 3/8" x 2 1/2" x 3" PERCHES
13"
vent
45° slope
3"
6"
1/2
6"
1/2
6"
1/2
5 1/2"
1/2
5 1/2"
3/4"
vent
SECTION
2 1/2"
2 1/2" entrance
ELEVATION
20"
1/2"
6"
6"
6"
6"
1/2"
1/2"
vent
PLAN - 1st FLOOR
Note: Floors, partitions & bottom are built in one unit. Side walls & roof are built in one unit, and lift off for cleaning. Units are fastened together by screws thru bottom into sides.
13 1/2"
6"
6"
1/2"
vent
13 1/2"
PLAN TOP FLOOR

NOW THAT YOU HAVE BUILT A BIRDHOUSE

If the birdhouse you've made is a work of art that's too beautiful to give to the birds, you can skip this section.

If your birdhouse is headed outside to house birds and age gracefully in the elements, you should read this section.

LOCATION

You may be wondering where to put the birdhouse how that's it's built. This is a good question to ponder as you look at your yard.

Where you put your birdhouse is as important as its design and construction. Birds are drawn to a particular habitat, and if your birdhouse is not in the right habitat, the birds you want to attract probably will not find it.

There are a number of things you can do to change your yard into an inviting habitat for birds. Feeders, birdbaths and fruit-bearing shrubs all make life easier for birds and can help make your yard into a good habitat.

Some birds need to be near bodies of water. Wood ducks and purple martins are in this category. Screech owls like to live at the edges of open fields.

There's only so much you can do to a yard to make a habitat, and trying to attract birds to an inappropriate habitat is a long shot at best.

A better strategy is to identify which birds already think your yard is a good habitat and build houses for them.

There are a few sure bets. Just about any yard that's not in the middle of a desert or near the arctic circle can attract titmice, wrens and chickadees.

PLACEMENT WITHIN THE HABITAT

First, you'll want to place the birdhouse where it will be away from people. Birds like their privacy so don't be surprised if you don't get any tenants if you place the house right beside your bedroom window.

You must also consider the recommended height above the ground as listed in the *Birdhouse Sizing Guide*.

Birds, like most animals, are territorial and need a bit of distance between them and the other birds that compete for the same food. The exception to this rule is the purple martin which prefers to nest in close proximity to other purple martins.

Although I put multiple-room chickadee houses in the *Ready to Use Plans* section, it is most likely that only one chickadee family will occupy the house at a time. The multiple rooms are there because the space is there.

Your chickadees may favor one of the rooms because of its orientation toward the sun or wind.

- Use no more than four small birdhouses
  for any one species or one large birdhouse per acre.

- Put about 100 yards between bluebird
  houses and 75 yards between swallow
  houses (if you have both species, "pair"
  the houses with one bluebird house 25
  feet from a swallow house. Put the "pair"
  100 yards away.)

- Don't put birdhouses near bird feeders. It
  is a good idea to have feeders somewhere in the habitat, just not too close to
  the birdhouses.

- Don't put more than one birdhouse in a
  tree, unless the tree is extremely large or
  the houses are for different species.

- If you have hot summers, face the entrance holes north or east to avoid over-
  heating the birdhouse.

- Most birds start thinking about nesting in
  late February to early March.

Some specific placement guidelines:

- Bluebirds like houses located 3 to 5 feet
  off the ground on stumps and fence posts
  near open fields such as golf courses,
  parks and cemeteries.

- Chickadees, nuthatches and titmice like
  houses mounted about 5 to 6 feet off the
  ground in wooded areas.

- Brown creepers and prothonotary warblers like heavily wooded areas and natural houses. Prothonotary warblers like
  their houses over water.

- Wrens will build nests in several boxes
  and are easy to attract. They don't mind
  suspended houses which sway in the
  wind, nor do they mind being close to
  people houses. Hang wren houses at eye
  level.

- Tree swallows prefer nest boxes attached to dead trees near bodies of water. Violet green swallows like nest
  boxes attached to large trees in semi-
  open woodland.

- Purple martins nest in groups and will
  readily take to multiple room houses.
  They generally nest fairly close to water
  and like plenty of airspace around the
  house (at least 40 feet) for orbits and
  flybys.

- Flycatchers like birdhouses which are
  about 10 feet up in trees in orchards or
  at the edge of fields and streams.

- Woodpeckers – specifically the flicker
  and red bellied – like birdhouses which
  are placed high on a tree trunk exposed
  to direct sunlight.

- Owls will nest in boxes mounted about
  15 feet up on a tree trunk near open
  fields or neglected orchards.

PLACEMENT FOR DECORATIVE EFFECT

If you are more interested in expressing yourself by building a birdhouse than in housing a particular bird, you will probably want to place your birdhouse where it will be admired.

Placing a birdhouse in such a way does not automatically mean it will not attract birds. It may just attract different birds than the ones you had in mind when you sized the house.

If you are displaying your birdhouse for decorative effect, you might want to consider creating a small "sky village" made up of several birdhouses mounted on poles along an invisible "sky street." This is an interesting visual effect, especially if your birdhouses look like real buildings and are in the same scale.

March 6, 1969. H. E. (Sam) Hubbard and a "sky village" he built to look like the famous Front Street of Dodge City, Kansas. The houses are designed to accommodate eight families of Purple Martins and weigh about 100 pounds each. They are mounted 15 feet off of the ground and stretch 40 feet from end to end. Mr. Hubbard donated the houses to his home town of Monett, Missouri, where they were placed in the City Park near the children's playground.

Mr. Hubbard built this birdhouse which is very similar to the Dodge City birdhouses on the previous page. His birdhouses are made of plywood and feature add-on windows as described on page 43.

SAM HUBBARD: A MASTER BIRDHOUSE BUILDER

Sam Hubbard hadn't worked with wood until he retired from the Frisco Railway in 1960. By 1974, he had built over 2000 birdhouses, most of which he gave to friends throughout the United States.

Mr. Hubbard also built several hundred leather-covered chests, grandfather clocks, and "all kinds of stuff for the kids in the neighborhood." Working without blueprints or plans, Mr. Hubbard built as his inspiration directed him.

When asked why he never took money for his creations, he said: "Well, if I did that, I would soon run out of customers; if you give them away, you never run out of customers."

A detail from the Monett School birdhouse

PROTECTION FROM PREDATORS

How and where you mount your birdhouse will determine how vulnerable your birds are to predators.

Houses mounted on posts and poles are the most difficult for predators to reach, especially if you use predator guards or smear poles with axle grease.

For details on how to build a predator guard, see the *Predator Guard Techniques* section on page 132.

The following animals are known to prey on nesting birds:

- Dogs are a hazard to nestlings in the spring and summer. Don't let your dog run loose during nesting time.

- House sparrows and starlings will bully or even kill nesting birds and their young. The best defense is to keep the entrance hole as small as you can for the species you want to attract and eliminate perches from your birdhouse.

- Insects often lay eggs and pupate in birdhouses. Watch your birdhouse for signs of bees, wasps, gypsy moths, blow flies, gnats and ants. If you suspect any of these have nested in the birdhouse, remove the insects. You can discourage bees and wasps by coating the inside of the roof with bar soap. In areas where gypsy moths abound, avoid placing birdhouses in oak trees, which are favored by gypsy moths. Insecticides should be avoided as they can harm the birds.

- Raccoons and Opossums will stick their arms inside birdhouses and try to pull out the adult, young and eggs. Adding a predator guard to the entrance hole of the birdhouse or to its mounting post or pole is a simple solution.

- House wrens will sometimes interfere with the nesting success of other birds by puncturing their eggs. Again, keep the entrance hole as small as possible and eliminate perches from birdhouses. Wrens are protected by law and must not be disturbed.

- Squirrels, red and sometimes gray, can become a serious menace to birdhouses and the birds themselves. Squirrels will find ways to get inside the birdhouse and eat the eggs and young. If you find the entrance hole enlarged, a red squirrel is probably at work. To discourage squirrels, add a predator guard of sheet metal to the entrance hole.

- Snakes can be deterred by putting the birdhouse on a metal pole smeared with petroleum jelly or cayenne pepper.

- Cats are notorious for raiding birds as they nest and roost. Being expert tree climbers, cats can usually get to birdhouses in trees and on wooden posts unless predator guards are in place. A sheet metal guard or cone on a tree can deter some less agile cats, but the best solution is to mount the house on a post or pole with a large, sturdy guard in place.

"Who, me?"

PREDATOR GUARD TECHNIQUES

You can make your own predator guard or buy one wherever outdoor bird supplies are sold.

The Arm Guard is just a block of 3/4" thick wood which doubles the thickness of the wall around the entrance hole. This effectively prevents cats, 'coons and 'possums from reaching inside the house to pull out eggs and nestlings.

The Arm Guard is illustrated on page 27.

The Gnaw Shield is a piece of sheet metal placed around the entrance hole to make it difficult, unpleasant or impossible for squirrels to chew their way into a birdhouse.

The Cone is a piece of sheet metal formed into a cone that wraps around a mounting post, pole or tree.

The Ceiling is a piece of sheet metal or wood attached to a pole or post in a manner similar to the cone. The ceiling is flat and does not require a lot of effort to make.

The Sheath is a piece of sheet metal which wraps around a post, pole or tree. The sheath is less effective than the cone.

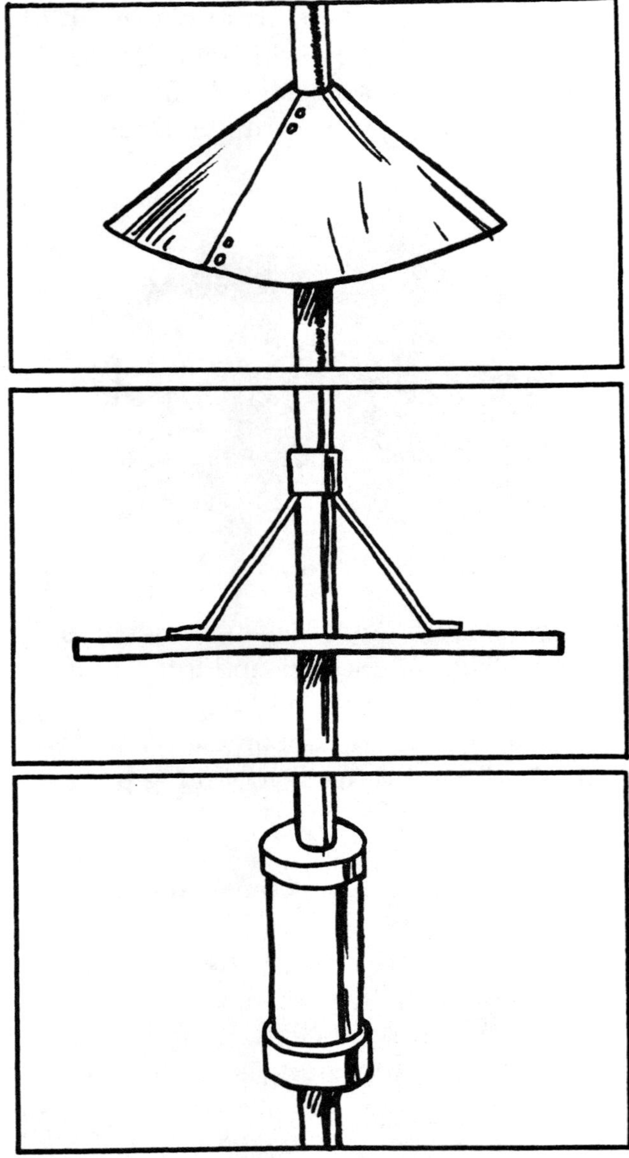

CREDITS

Production: Jeanne FitzPatrick, Barbara Murphy, John Morford, Boyd Maits, Robert T. Hubbard, Barbara Nislick, Bob DiLullo, David Molter, Lacey Simons, Carl Weiss, Rob Fleming

Cover: Sheriff-Krebs Design, Philadelphia

Photography: Pages 8, 9,14 and 133, American Primitive Gallery; Pages 10, 26 and 104, Malcolm Wells; Pages 117-119 and 121-123, Gladstone Califf; Page 128, Bettmann Archive; Page 129 Jerry Whitford

Cartoons: Pages 15, 45 and 53, Mark Tatulli

Drawings: Page 24, Evelyn Hartman, Pages 27 and 132, Mark Tatulli; Pages 29 and 117-125, Gladstone Califf; Pages 48 and 107-116, Malcolm Wells

FOR MORE INFORMATION:

GENERAL INFORMATION:

U.S. Fish and Wildlife Service
Department of the Interior
Washington, D.C. 20240

BIRDHOUSES AND SUPPLIES:

American Primitive Gallery
594 Broadway, Room 205
New York, NY 10012
212 966-1530
*One-of-a-kind antique and
folk-art birdhouses.*

Dakota Quality Bird Feed
Box 3084
Fargo, ND 58108
1 800 356-9220

Dilworthtown Country Store
275 Brintons Bridge Road
West Chester, PA 19382
610 399-0560
*Unique handmade birdhouses offered in
spring and summer. Birdhouse show
every spring.*

SUGGESTED READING:

A Field Guide to the Birds of North America by Robbins, Brunn, Zim, and
Singer. Golden Press, 1983.

The Audubon Society Guide to Attracting Birds by Stephen W. Kress.
Charles Scribner's Sons, 1985.

30 Birds That Will Nest in Birdhouses by R.B. Layton, Nature Book Publishing Company, 1977.

The Bluebird: How You Can Help Fight For Its Survival by Lawrence
Zeleny. Indiana University Press, 1976.

The New Handbook of Attracting Birds by Thomas P. McElroy, Jr. W.W.
Norton & Company, 1960.

Woodworking For Wildlife by Carrol Henderson. Minnesota Department of
Natural Resources, St. Paul, 1984.

Basic Carpentry Techniques by Ortho Books, 1981.

Classic Architectural Birdhouses and Feeders by Malcolm Wells. Published
by the author, 1988. Can be ordered from Radnor-Hill Publishing, Box 41051,
Phila, PA 19127; $9.95 + $3.50 S&H (2nd day delivery).

INDEX

Duck, wood   *see Wood duck*
Durability 21, 30, 43-44
Dust 39

E

Eggs
    bird 42, 131
    insect 131
Emotion 6, 11-12
English Cottage 121
Entrance hole 8, 15, 17, 27-28, 33, 52, 131-132
    techniques for making 33
Environment 10
    blending with 10, 54
Epoxy 19
Exterior grade plywood 21
Exterior paints 44
Eye hazards 25

F

Factory edges 31, 37
Fasteners 19
    see also Nails, Screws
File 23, 25, 33
Finish see Paint
Flashing 19, 41
Flea markets 8
Flicker 17
Flies 131
Floor 17, 29, 30, 34, 36-37, 39, 49-50, 52
    platform 30, 117-125
    recessed 30, 117
Floor stop blocks 36
Flycatcher 17, 127
Folk art 8, 9
Formula for making plans 50
Found wood 20-21, 92-94
Functional birdhouses 14

G

Garden 7, 13, 126
Gift shops 8, 9
Glass 43, 100-103

Glue
    types 19
    usage 35-36, 38, 58, 70, 80, 88, 94, 102
Gnats 131
Green Mountain Ranch 20, 41-42, 92-99
Gypsy moths 131

H

Habitat 15, 126-127
Hammer 23, 25, 35-37
Hand tools 6, 22-25
    usage of 31-43
Hangout 10, 108-110
Heat 19, 28, 42, 52, 127
Heirloom 7, 43
High design 10
History of birdhouse building 18
Hole saw 33
Hot melt glue 19
Hubbard, H.E. (Sam) 128-129

I

Imagination 7, 46-47
Individuality 8
Inner partition 36, 39
Insecticide 13, 131
Insects 131
Intersecting rooflines 40, 42, 92

J

Japanese Bluebird House 122

K

Knots 21

L

Labels on crates 21
Labels on plywood 18
Latex paint 44
Lattice 41, 43, 79, 87